Abandonment to Divine Providence

Posthumous Work
OF

Rev. J. P. de Caussade, S.J.

REVISED AND CORRECTED BY
Rev. H. Ramière, S.J.

Translated from the Eighth French Edition

By

Miss Ella McMahon.

Loki's Publishing

Contents

Preface
On The Foundation And True Nature Of The Virtue Of Abandonment,To Explain And Defend Father Caussade's Doctrine.

There is no truth however clear which does not become error the moment it is lessened or exaggerated; and there is no food however salutary for the soul which may not, when ill-applied, become a fatal poison.

The virtue of abandonment does not escape this danger; the more holy and profitable it is in itself the more serious are the dangers we risk by misunderstanding its just limits.

These dangers, unfortunately, are not mere possibilities. The seventeenth century witnessed the birth of a heresy,—that of the Quietists,—which, while claiming to teach its followers perfect abandonment to God, led them into the most terrible disorders. For a time this sect wrought its ravages in the very capital of Catholicism, and put forth such specious sophistries that the pious Fénelon himself, while abhorring the practical consequences drawn from this teaching, was for a time misled by its false appearance of perfection.

To preserve Father Caussade's readers from these dangers, we think it well to add to these writings a succinct exposition of the rules which should guide us in a matter so delicate. By the light of the principles jointly furnished us by reason and faith, we shall have no difficulty in determining the just limits which should mark our abandonment to divine Providence; and it will be easy for us afterwards to elucidate the points in our author's doctrine which might be wrongly interpreted.

I.

Father Caussade explains very clearly in his "Letters" the two principles which form the unalterable basis of the virtue of abandonment.

First principle: Nothing is done, nothing happens, either in the material or in the moral world, which God has not foreseen from all eternity, and which He has not willed, or at least permitted.

Second principle: God can will nothing, He can permit nothing, but in view of the end He proposed to Himself in creating the world; *i.e.*, in view of His glory and the glory of the Man-God, Jesus Christ, His only Son.

To these two principles laid down by our author we shall add a third, which will complete the elucidation of this whole subject: As long as man lives upon earth, God desires to be glorified through the happiness of this privileged creature; and consequently in God's designs the interest of man's sanctification and happiness is inseparable from the interest of the divine glory.

If we do not lose sight of these principles, which no Christian can question, we shall understand that our confidence in the Providence of our Father in heaven cannot be too great, too absolute, too childlike. If nothing but what He permits happens, and if He can permit nothing but what is for our happiness, then we have nothing to fear, except not being sufficiently submissive to God. As long as we keep ourselves united with Him and we walk after His designs, were all creatures to turn against us they could not harm us. He who relies upon God becomes by this very reliance as powerful and as invincible as God, and created powers can no more prevail against him than against God Himself.

This confidence in the fatherly providence of God cannot, evidently, dispense us from doing all that is in our power to accomplish His designs; but after having done all that depends upon our efforts we will abandon ourselves completely to God for the rest.

This abandonment should extend, in fact, to everything—to the past, to the present, to the future; to the body and all its conditions; to the soul and all its miseries, as well as all its qualities; to blessings; to afflictions; to the good will of men, and to their malice; to the vicissitudes of the material, and the revolutions of the moral, world; to life and to death; to time and to eternity.

However, as these different orders of things do not enter in the same manner in the designs of divine Providence, neither should our abandonment in regard to these be practised in the same manner; and the rules which we should follow in the practice of this virtue should be founded on the nature itself of the objects which call it forth. We shall indicate the principal ones.

I. Among all the dispositions to which our abandonment can be applied, there are first, those which depend solely upon God, where human liberty has no part either in producing or averting them. Such are, for example, certain scourges, and vicissitudes of the atmosphere; certain accidents impossible to foresee, certain natural defects of body or soul.

In regard to facts of this order, whether of the past, present, or future, it is evident that our abandonment cannot be too absolute.

There is nothing to do here but to passively and lovingly endure all that God sends us; to blindly accept in advance all that it may please Him to send us in the future. Resistance would be useless, and only serve to make us unhappy; a loving and frequently renewed acceptance, on the contrary, would make these inevitable sufferings very meritorious. And oh, the marvels of God's goodness! Our abandonment will not only sanctify and fructify real trials; it will enable us to derive great merit from trials to which we shall never be subjected. For, if we lovingly accept these trials when they present themselves to our minds as probable, or simply possible, this willing acquiescence, this *fiat* uttered in the depths of the heart, cannot fail to please God, and be very useful to our souls. Therefore, in regard to this first order of events, the practice of abandonment cannot but be very sanctifying, as it changes into means of sanctification not only real but even purely imaginary trials.

II. There are other sufferings which come to us through the malice of creatures: persecutions, calumnies, ill-treatment, neglect, injustice, and offences of every kind. What are we to do when we find ourselves exposed to vexatious things of this sort?

1st. We evidently cannot like the offence against God with which they are accompanied; we should, on the contrary, deplore and detest it, not because it wounds our self-love, but because it is an offence against the divine rights, and compromises the salvation of the offending souls.

2d. As for that which concerns us, on the contrary, we should regard as a blessing that which is in itself an evil; and to do this we need only recall the principles previously laid down: not to look only at the creature who is the immediate cause of our sufferings, but to raise our eyes higher and behold God, who has foreseen and permitted them from all eternity, and who in permitting them had only our happiness in view. This thought will be sufficient to dissipate the bitterness and trouble which would take possession of our hearts were we to lok only at the injustice of which we are the victims.

3d. In regard to the effects of this injustice already consummated and irreparable, we have only to resign ourselves as lovingly as possible, and carefully gather their precious fruits. It is frequently not difficult to divine the spiritual fruits God destined for us in exposing us to temporal evils: to detach us from creatures; to deliver us from inordinate affections, from our pride, from our tepidity,—veritable maladies of the soul, frequently all the more dangerous that they are less perceptible, and of which the heavenly Physician wishes to cure us, using the malice of our neighbor as a sharp instrument. We do not hesitate to endure much greater sufferings to be delivered from corporal infirmities; then let us gratefully accept the spiritual health, infinitely more precious, which God offers us, however disagreeable the instrument through which He gives it to us.

4th. If it is in our power to avert the consequences of malice and injustice, and if in our true interest, and in the interest of the divine glory, we deem it necessary to take any measures to this end, let us do so without departing from the practice of the holy virtue of abandonment. Let us commit the success of our efforts to God, and be ready to accept failure if God judges it more suitable to His designs and more profitable to our souls. We are so blind that we always have reason to fear being deceived; but God cannot be deceived, and we may be certain, in advance, that what He determines will be best. Therefore we cannot do better than abandon with fullest confidence the result of our efforts to Him.

III. But should this abandonment extend equally to our acts of imprudence, to our faults, and all the annoyances of every kind in which they may result?

It is important to distinguish here two things which self-love tends to confound. In the fault itself we must distinguish what is culpable and what is humiliating. Likewise in its consequences we must distinguish what is detrimental to the divine glory and the confusion inflicted on our self-love. Evidently we cannot hate too much the fault, properly so called, nor regret too keenly the injury done to the divine glory. But as for our humiliation, and the confusion inflicted on our self-love, we should rejoice, and acquiesce in it with complete abandonment. This kind of sacrifice is undoubtedly the best fitted to destroy in us the most secret fibres of self-love, and to cause us to make rapid progress in virtue. To souls who have attained a certain degree of regularity and detachment, exterior humiliations are very little. When we have learned the vanity of human glory, we easily endure the sting of contempt; but we may still unite with this exterior detachment great attachment to our own esteem and approbation, and a wholly egotistical desire of perfection. In this case, self-love, by changing its object, would only become more subtle and more dangerous. To destroy it, there is no remedy more efficacious than the humiliation resulting from our faults; and we cannot, consequently, strive too earnestly to apply the practice of abandonment to this humiliation, endeavoring at the same time to correct the faults themselves.

And what we say of faults of the past applies equally to faults of the future. The practice of abandonment well understood should deliver us from that impatience which makes us wish to at once attain the summit of perfection, and which only serves to keep us from it by turning us from the only path which leads to perfection. This path is humility, and the impatience which we are censuring is only another form of pride. Let us make every effort to correct our faults; but let us be resigned to not seeing them all disappear in a day. Let us earnestly, and with the most filial confidence, ask God to grant us that decisive grace which will completely wrest us from ourselves, to make us live only in Him; but let us leave to Him, with an equally filial abandonment, the care of determining the day and hour in which this grace shall be given us.

With still greater reason should we abandon to God the determining of the degree of sanctity which we shall attain upon earth, the extraordinary graces which will accompany this sanctity here below, and the glory with which it will be crowned in heaven. In as far as it depends upon us, we should leave nothing undone to increase this sanctity and this glory, in order not to fall short of the degree God has marked for us; but if we must earnestly devote ourselves to realizing His designs, we must not desire to have them other than they are. If our love for God is what it should be, we will thank Him for having granted other souls favors that He has refused us, and we will praise Him no less for our poverty than for our riches.

IV. Should our abandonment go still farther? Should we, in view of the hypothesis—perfectly possible, alas!—of our damnation, resign ourselves thereto, and thus make to God the complete and absolute sacrifice of all our own interests?

To this point would Fénelon have carried the purity of love and the perfection of abandonment; and he did not lack plausible motives with which to support this doctrine. He drew from the example and the writings of the Saints arguments still more specious to prove that God frequently requires this complete sacrifice of elect souls; and that to obtain it He impresses them with an irresistible conviction of their eternal loss. According to this great prelate, divine love is only perfect in souls who have gone through this trial without faltering, and who by a sacrifice have renounced, at least hypothetically, all their own interest, even that of their eternal salvation.

But the Church has condemned this doctrine which, in proposing to man a perfection contrary to his nature, reverses the order of God's designs. How, in fact, can perfection consist in destroying the most essential law of our moral nature, viz., that irresistible inclination which leads us to seek our happiness? How could love of God require that we rob God of one of His attributes—the one which makes Him the supreme object of our beatitude? How could one of the theological virtues be contrary to another, and charity exclude hope? What is eternal happiness if not the eternal reign of pure love? and how could the pure love of time consist in excluding, even hypothetically, from our desires the pure love of eternity?

That which perfect abandonment asks is that we observe in our desires the order of God's designs. God created all things for His glory first; and secondly, but inseparably, for our happiness. Let us do as He does: let us never separate the interest of His glory from that of our happiness, but let us always make the second subordinate to the first. Let us love God as the object of our beatitude, but let us love Him above all for His infinite goodness. Let us desire and hope for our eternal happiness; but since this happiness, when we shall enjoy it, must result from the love of God for Himself, let us begin now to seek it as it must be when we realize it, and refer the desire of it, as we will one day refer its enjoyment, to the glory of this great God who desires to be all in all things.

Thus, at one and the same time, we can practise charity and hope, seek the glory of God and our own happiness, fill the designs of our Creator, and satisfy the deepest and most imperative needs of our nature.

The saints did not do otherwise; and Father Caussade, in one of his letters, proves very clearly that the formulas of apparent despair that they have sometimes used in the transports of their cruel sufferings contained in reality acts of the most meritorious confidence. Elsewhere he also shows most perfectly how ill-founded is this even hypothetic separation between God's interests and our true interests; and he justly concludes therefrom that perfection cannot consist in supposing this separation and sacrificing the interest of our eternal happiness to that of the divine glory.

II.

We have no reason, therefore, to fear that in reading Father Caussade's treatise we are liable to confound, at least in this respect, the abandonment he recommends with the Quietism condemned in Fénelon.

Is our author equally irreproachable in all the other points of his doctrine? Might he not be accused of turning his readers from duties which require labor and effort to keep them in an indolent repose?

There would be ground for this reproach if Father Caussade promised to give his readers a complete treatise on Christian and religious perfection; but this he does not do. He addresses himself to souls already advanced in virtue and accustomed not only to faithfully fulfil the essential precepts of Christianity, but also to observe the prescriptions of religious discipline. Like the young man in the Gospel who from his youth had kept the commandments, and who begged our Saviour to show him a higher perfection, these souls ask Father Caussade what they must do to sanctify themselves after having accomplished all the duties imposed upon their free will. The man of God answers them like our Saviour: If you would be perfect, rid yourself of all that may still cling to you of attachment to your own interests, your own ideas, your own will, and abandon yourself completely to God. Practise the virtue of abandonment; practise it so habitually that it will become the constant state of your soul: thus you will cease to live to yourself, to live only in God.

This is a summary of the book we are re-editing to-day. To understand it we must bear in mind, as we read it, the situation of the author, and that of the souls to whom his counsels are addressed; viz., that it is not, as we have already said, a complete treatise of Christian perfection which he has claimed to write; his only object was to set forth the advantages of a special virtue and a particular state. It is true that this virtue is one of the most essential bases of sanctity, and that this state is sanctity itself as far as it is attainable on earth. But it is no less true that Father Caussade had no idea whatever of telling all Christians what they should do to save their souls. Therefore it would be a serious mistake to believe ourselves dispensed from all duties of which he makes no mention, in order to devote ourselves only to this great duty of abandonment, the importance of which he so justly and eloquently portrays.

To avoid this dangerous error, and reap all the profit of this true and very consoling doctrine of Father Caussade, it will be sufficient to cast a general glance over the divine economy in the salvation of souls, and to see what place abandonment to divine Providence occupies in this great work.

We all know that sanctification is a work both divine and human. It is divine through its immediate principle, the Holy Spirit; through its meritorious cause, the Incarnation and the death of the Son of God; through its end, the happiness of the Holy Trinity, in which holy souls are to participate for all eternity; finally, through its chief means, the teachings and the graces of Jesus Christ transmitted to men through the Church.

But this work is human also, since the graces of the Holy Spirit, the merits of the Son of God, the designs of the Holy Trinity, and all the efforts of Providence can bear fruit in a soul only as far as she freely co-operates with them.

This co-operation in our sanctification which God requires of us is composed of three parts.

It consists first of all in the destruction of everything in our corrupt nature which is an obstacle to the divine action: sins, vices, sensible inclinations, defects, imperfections. This first labor is what the masters of the spiritual life call the *purgative way*. It is accomplished by examinations of conscience, works of penance and mortification, and the various practices in use in the Church.

The second part of the labor which God imposes on the soul desirous to attain sanctity is less painful, and easier. It is what is called the *illuminative way*. The soul that God introduces therein exercises herself in producing the interior acts of virtue with which grace inspires her, and in practicing the good works to which this same grace impels her.

Finally, when the obstacles are removed and the soul's preparation is completed, God unites Himself to her, fills her with His grace, inflames her with His love, and uses her as a docile instrument for the accomplishment of His designs: this is the *unitive way*.

But let us not misapprehend this condition. Even in this perfect state in which God is fully master of His reasonable creature, He does not act in her without her co-operation; He requires of her great fidelity in avoiding the smallest faults, great vigilance over her affections, great generosity in denying herself in all things, great fervor in prayer. So far from dispensing her from the works of the illuminative way by which she prepared herself for the divine union, He causes her to accomplish them with greater perfection and merit.

Among these works common to the two ways of which we have just spoken, there are some which are strictly of obligation, either because they are prescribed to all Christians by the commandments of God and the Church, or because they are imposed on each one by the special circumstances of his state. There are others which are simply of counsel, or even purely of supererogation, and which each one embraces according to his more or less ardent desire of sanctification. In the same way, among the works of penance which form the purgative way there are some from which no one can dispense himself; but there are others which, without being of absolute necessity, are more or less useful, or even relatively necessary to certain souls, because of their particular position, and the violence of the inclinations which impel them to evil.

Such is man's threefold part in the beginning, progress, and consummation of the eminently divine work of sanctification— a part essentially active, and so necessary that without it God's part would be hopelessly sterile. Father Caussade, however, says very little of it in his book. Does he doubt its immense importance and absolute necessity? Far from it. On the contrary, in many passages he is careful to warn us that the *passiveness* which he recommends to the soul in no way dispenses her from the very active accomplishment of all that is *duty*, whether general or special. He adds that the souls who walk in the ordinary ways should not dispense themselves from the practices of supererogation in use in the Church among pious persons, and from following the rules traced by the masters of the spiritual life. Even upon persons who have reached the passive state he imposes the obligation of actively following the inspirations of grace when they lead to action, and of doing all to which they are impelled by grace.

Why, then, after making these reservations in some parts of his work does he seem to forget them, to solely extol the advantages of abandonment to the divine action? We have already said why: because the souls to whom he addressed himself, long exercised in the practice of active virtue, had special need to perfect themselves in this passive abandonment.

How many such souls there are in religious communities, or even in the midst of the world, who have no need to be urged to activity in the pursuit of sanctity, but who, on the contrary, need above all things to learn to let God act in them! Father Caussade addresses himself specially to these souls. Had his book no other result than to enlighten them upon God's real designs concerning them, to deliver them from their disquieting agitation in order to introduce them into a broad and peaceful path, and enable them to find powerful means of salvation in unfortuitous events which they regard as obstacles, we should still believe that in offering this work to them we are doing them an eminent service.

But the salutary teaching of this book is not limited to a special class of persons. Though written specially for souls who have already attained a high degree of perfection, the doctrine it develops is suited to all Christians. It makes it clear to all that if God does not dispense them from laboring actively for their salvation, He takes upon Himself the greatest part of this work; that He unceasingly labors thereon; that He employs all creatures and all events to further it; and that if they will only permit Him to do His will,—without doing any more than they are doing, without suffering any more than they are suffering, but only by recognizing and loving God's action in things which He obliges them to do and suffer, they will amass infinite merits and attain great perfection.

Thus Father Caussade does not suppress our active co-operation in the work of our sanctification, but he teaches us to profit much better than we do of God's part therein, by abandoning ourselves more to Him. In events where too frequently we see only misfortunes, because we regard them as more or less reprehensible effects of the malice or the imperfection of creatures, he teaches us to see the divine love using these same creatures as instruments either to correct our vices or to cause us to practise virtue. Therefore he changes the principal obstacles to the success of this great work into means of sanctification, and teaches us the art of changing creatures the most indifferent or the most hostile into powerful auxiliaries. With good reason does he desire to be able to inculcate this doctrine in men of all conditions; for there is no doubt that, if they understood it well, sanctity would seem to them much more attainable; and that, seeing God laboring unceasingly upon this work, they would fulfil with much greater courage the duties imposed upon their free will.

H. Ramière, S.J.

Book First.
The Nature and Excellence of the Virtue of Holy Abandonment.

CHAPTER I.

The Sanctity of the Righteous of the Old Law, and of Joseph and of Mary herself, consisted in Fidelity to the Order of God.

God speaks to-day as He spoke to our fathers, when directors were not so numerous, nor methods of direction so well defined. All their spirituality consisted in simple fidelity to the order of God; but it was not reduced to a science which explained it so sublimely or minutely, or contained so many precepts, so many maxims, so much instruction. Our present wants, no doubt, require this explanation. It was not so in the first ages of the Church, when men were more simple and upright. Each moment brought a duty to be faithfully fulfilled: this was sufficient for interior souls of that day. Their whole attention was concentrated simply upon the duty of each successive moment with the fidelity of the hour-hand of a clock which steadily traverses stroke by stroke the circle in which it is appointed to move. The mind, unceasingly moved by divine grace, turned insensibly to the new duty which presented itself in the order of God every hour. Such were the hidden springs of Mary's life, the most perfect example of simple and absolute self-abandonment to the will of God. The simple words, *Fiat mihi secundum verbum tuum*, with which she was content to answer the angel, expressed all the mystic theology of the ancients. Then, as now, it was all reduced to the simplest and most absolute abandonment of the soul to the will of God under whatever form it manifested itself. This noble and exalted disposition, the basis of all Mary's spirituality, is brilliantly manifested in the words *Fiat mihi.* Observe how perfectly they accord with those which our Lord would have ever on our lips and in our hearts: *Fiat voluntas tua.* True, the duty required of Mary at that supreme moment was a glorious one for her. But all the splendor of that glory would have made no impression upon her if the divine will, alone capable of influencing her, had not arrested her attention. It was this divine will which guided her in everything. Her occupations, whether ordinary or exalted, were in her eyes but shadows more or less obscure in which she found equal means of glorifying God and recognizing the workings of the Almighty. She joyfully accepted the duty or suffering of each moment as a gift from Him who fills with good things the hearts which are nourished by Him alone, and not by appearances or created things.

CHAPTER II.

The Duties of each Moment are the Shadows which veil the Divine Action.

"The power of the Most High shall overshadow thee," said the angel to Mary.

This shadow, behind which the power of God effects the entrance and growth of Jesus Christ in our souls, is the form assumed by the duties, attractions, and crosses of each moment.

They are in truth but shadows like those to which we give the name in the order of nature, and which envelop sensible objects and hide them from our view. Thus in the moral and supernatural order the duties of each moment under their obscure appearances conceal the truth of the divine will, which alone merits our attention. Thus Mary regarded them. Therefore these shadows passing before her senses, so far from deceiving her, filled her with faith in Him who is always the same. Withdraw, Archangel; thy moment passes; thou vanishest. Mary passes beyond thee; she is ever in advance; but the Holy Ghost, with whom she has been filled through the sensible appearances of thy mission, will never abandon her.

There are few extraordinary events in the exterior life of Mary. At least it is not to these that Holy Scripture calls our attention. Her exterior life is represented as very simple, very ordinary. She did and suffered as did others of her condition. She goes to visit her cousin Elizabeth: the other relatives go also. She retires to a stable: it is a consequence of her poverty. She returns to Nazareth: the persecution of Herod had driven her forth. Jesus and Joseph lived there with her, by the labor of their hands. Behold the daily bread of the holy family! But with what bread was the faith of Mary and Joseph nourished? What was the sacrament of all their sacred moments? What did they discover under the ordinary appearance of the events which filled their lives? Exteriorly, nothing more than was happening to the rest of mankind; interiorly, faith discovers and develops nothing less than God working great things. O bread of angels! Heavenly manna! Pearl of the Gospel! Sacrament of the present moment! Thou givest God under appearances as poor and mean as the manger, the hay, and the straw! But to whom dost thou give Him? *Esurientes reples bonis.* God reveals Himself to the humble in little things; and the proud, regarding only the exterior, find Him not even in great things.

CHAPTER III.

How much Easier Sanctity becomes when studied from this Point of View.

If the work of our salvation offers obstacles apparently so insurmountable, it is because we have not a just idea of it. In truth, sanctity consists in but one thing—fidelity to the order of God; and this fidelity is equally within the reach of all, whether in its active or in its passive part.

The active part of fidelity consists in fulfilling the duties imposed upon us either by the general commands of God and the Church, or by the particular state we have embraced.

Its passive part consists in lovingly accepting all that God sends us each moment.

Which of these two parts of sanctity is above our strength? Not the active part, since the duties it enjoins cease to be duties for us the moment our strength is really unequal to them. Will not the state of your health permit you to hear Mass? You are no longer obliged to do so. And so it is with all positive obligations which prescribe duties to be fulfilled. Only those precepts which forbid things evil in themselves admit of no exception, for it is never permitted to do evil.

Is there anything easier or more reasonable? What excuse can be urged against it? Yet this is all the co-operation God requires of the soul in the work of its sanctification.

He requires it of great and small, of strong and weak; in a word, of all, at all times, in all places.

Therefore He only requires of us what is easy, since to attain eminent sanctity requires but a simple good-will.

If over and above the commandments He shows us the counsels as the more perfect end of our efforts, He is ever careful to accommodate their observance to our position and character. As the chief mark of our vocation for the counsels He sends us the attractions and graces which facilitate the practice of them. He urges no one but in proportion to his strength and according to his attainments. Again I ask, what could be more just?

O you who aspire to perfection and are tempted to discouragement by what you read in the lives of the saints and find prescribed in certain pious books! O you who are overwhelmed by the terrible ideas that you form of perfection! It is for your consolation that God permits that I write this.

Learn what you seem not to know.

In the order of nature, necessary things, as air, water, earth, the God of all goodness has made common and easy of attainment. Nothing is more necessary than breath, sleep, food, and nothing is more common. Love and fidelity are no less necessary in the spiritual order; therefore the difficulty of acquiring them cannot be as great as you represent it to yourselves.

Observe your life; of what does it consist? Of a multitude of unimportant actions. Yet with these same unimportant actions God deigns to be content. This is the co-operation required of the soul in the work of its perfection. God Himself expresses it too clearly to admit of doubt: "Fear God, and keep His commandments: for this is all man" (Eccles. xii. 13). That is to say, this is all that is required on man's part; in this consists his active fidelity. Let him fulfil his part; God will do the rest. Grace, working by itself, effects marvels which surpass the intelligence of man. For ear has not heard, eye has not seen, heart has not felt, what God conceives in His mind, resolves in His will, executes by His power in souls wholly abandoned to Him.

The passive part of sanctity is still easier, since it consists in accepting what very often we cannot avoid, and bearing with love, that is, with consolation and sweetness, what we too frequently endure with weariness and irritation. Again let me repeat, herein lies all sanctity. It is the grain of mustard-seed the fruits of which we do not gather, because we fail to recognize it in its littleness. It is the drachma of the Gospel, the treasure which we do not find, do not seek, because we imagine it too far beyond us.

Ask me not the secret of finding this treasure, for secret there is none. This treasure is everywhere; it is offered to all, at all times, in all places.

Through creatures, friends, and enemies it flows plentifully; it flows over the faculties of our bodies, of our souls, and into the very centre of our hearts. Let us but open our mouths and they will be filled. The divine action floods the universe; it penetrates all creatures; it floats above them, about them; it is ever present with them; it precedes them; it accompanies them; it follows them, and they have but to allow themselves to be borne onward on its tide.

Would to God kings and their ministers, princes of the Church and of the world, priests, soldiers, peasants, laborers, in a word, all men, knew how easily they can attain eminent sanctity! They have but to fulfil the simple duties of religion and their state in life, and bear with submission the crosses these duties bring, and accept with faith and love the work and suffering which unsought and unceasingly come to them through the order of Providence. This is the spirituality which sanctified the patriarchs and prophets before there were so many methods and so many masters in the spiritual life.[1]

This is the spirituality of all ages and of all states, which cannot be more surely sanctified, or in a manner more noble, more extraordinary, more easy, than by the simple use of that which God, the Sovereign Director of souls, gives them each moment to do or suffer.

---

[1] It would be a gross misapprehension of the author's words to suppose that he wishes to urge souls to enter the paths of the spiritual life without a director. He himself expressly states elsewhere that to be able to do without a director, one must have been long and skilfully directed. Still less does he wish to discourage the practices adopted by the Church for the extirpation of vice and the acquisition of virtue. What he desires to say, and what we cannot impress too much upon Christians, is that the first of all directions is the guidance of Providence, and that the most necessary and the most perfect of all practices is the faithful accomplishment and loving acceptance of all that this fatherly Providence sends us to do and suffer.

CHAPTER IV.

Perfection does not consist in knowing the Order of God, but in submitting to it.

The order of God, the good pleasure of God, the will of God, the action of God, the grace of God, all these are one and the same thing in this life. It is God laboring to render the soul like unto Him. Perfection is nothing but the soul's faithful co-operation in this labor of God. This work is silently effected in our souls, where it thrives, increases, and is consummated unconsciously to ourselves.

Theology is full of conceptions and expressions which explain the wonders of this work effected in individual souls according to their capacity.

We may know all the theory of this work, admirably write and speak thereon, and instruct and direct souls; but if our knowledge be only theoretical, then I say that in comparison with souls which live and act by the order of God and are guided by His divine will, though ignorant of the theory of its operations or its different effects, and unable to speak thereof, we are like a sick physician compared to ordinary persons in perfect health.

The order of God, His divine will, received with simplicity by a faithful soul, effects this divine work in her unconsciously to herself, just as a remedy submissively taken restores the health of a sick man, although he have not, and need not have, any knowledge of medicine.

It is the fire which warms us, and not the philosophical knowledge of the element and its effects; so it is the order of God, His divine will, and not the curious speculation on its principles and its methods, which produces the sanctification of our souls.

If we thirst, we must drink; theoretical explanations will not quench our thirst. Curiosity for knowledge only makes us thirst still more. Therefore, if we thirst for sanctification, curious speculations only keep us farther from it. We must abandon all theories and drink in simplicity of all that the will of God sends us of work and suffering.

That which comes to us each moment by the order of God is best and holiest and most divine for us.

CHAPTER V.

Reading and other Exercises only sanctify us in so far as they are the Channels of the Divine Action.

All our science consists in recognizing God's will in regard to the present moment. All reading pursued in any other spirit than that of submission to the order of God is injurious. The will of God, the order of God, is the grace which works in the depths of our hearts by means of our readings and by all our other works. Without it our readings are but shadows, vain appearances, which, coming to us devoid of the vivifying virtue of the order of God, serve only to empty the heart by the very plenitude they cause in the mind.

The virtue of this divine will flowing into the soul of a simple, ignorant girl by means of suffering or ordinary actions, effects in the depths of her heart this mysterious work of the supernatural Being without filling her mind with any idea likely to awaken pride; while the proud man who studies spiritual books only through curiosity, and does not unite his reading to the will of God, receives into his mind the letter without the spirit, and becomes colder and more hardened than ever.

The order of God, His divine will, is the life of the soul under whatever appearances the soul receives it or applies it to herself.

Whatever may be the relation of the divine will to the mind, it nourishes the soul, and unceasingly strengthens her growth by giving her each moment what is best for her. Nor is one thing more efficacious than another in producing these happy effects; no, it is simply the duty of the present moment which comes to us by the order of God. That which was best for us in the past moment is no longer best for us, for it is stripped of the will of God, which has passed on to other things from which it creates for us the duty of the present moment; and it is this duty, under whatever appearance it is manifested, which will now most perfectly sanctify our souls.

If the divine will make reading the duty of the present moment, the reading will effect His mysterious work in the depths of the soul. If, in obedience to the divine will, we leave the reading for the duty of contemplation, this duty will create the new man in the depths of the heart, and reading would then be injurious and useless. If the divine will withdraw us from contemplation to hear confessions or to other duties, and that during a considerable time, these duties form Jesus Christ in the depths of the heart, and all the sweetness of contemplation would only serve to banish Him.

The order of God is the fulness of all our moments. It flows under a thousand different appearances which, successively becoming our present duty, form, increase, and complete the new man in us, in all the fulness which the divine wisdom has destined for us. This mysterious growth of Jesus Christ in us is the work produced by the order of God; it is the fruit of His grace and of His divine will.

This fruit, as we have said, is germinated, increased, and nourished by the succession of our present duties filled with the virtue of this same divine will.

In fulfilling these duties we are always sure of possessing the "better part," for this holy will is itself the better part. We have but to yield to it, blindly abandon ourselves to it with perfect confidence. It is infinitely holy, infinitely wise, infinitely powerful, for souls which unreservedly hope in it, which love and seek but it alone, and which believe with unfaltering faith that what it assigns to each moment is best without seeking elsewhere for more or less, and without pausing to consider the relation of material things with the order of God, which is the seeking of pure self-love.

The will of God is the essential, the reality and virtue, of all things; it is that which adapts and renders them suitable to the soul.

Without it all is emptiness, nothingness, falsehood, the empty husk, the letter without the spirit, vanity, death.

The will of God is the health, the life, the salvation of soul and body, whatever its manifestation or ways of reaching us.

Therefore we must not judge of the virtue of things by the relations they bear to mind or body, for these relations are unimportant. It is the will of God alone which gives to all things, whatever they may be, the power to form Jesus Christ in the depth of our hearts. We must frame no laws for this will and place no limit to its action, for it is all-powerful.

Whatever the ideas which fill the mind, whatever the feelings which the body experiences, were it for the mind but distractions and trouble, for the body but sickness and death, the divine will nevertheless is ever for the present moment the life of body and soul; for both one and the other, whatever their condition, are sustained by it alone. Bread without it is poison; and through it poison becomes a salutary remedy. Without it, books but confuse and trouble us; with it, darkness is turned into light. It is the wisdom, the truth, of all things. In all things it gives us God: and God is the infinite Being who holds the place of all things to the soul which possesses Him.

CHAPTER VI.

The Mind and other Human Means are Useful only in as far as they are the Instruments of the Divine Action.

The mind with all its powers would hold the first place among the instruments of the divine will; but it must, like a dangerous slave, be reduced to the last.

The simple of heart who know how to use it can derive great profit therefrom; but it can also do much injury when not kept in subjection.

When the soul sighs after created means, the divine action whispers to the heart that it sufficeth; when she would injudiciously reject them, the divine action whispers that they are instruments not to be taken or rejected at will, but to be simply received from Providence and adapted to the order of God—the soul thus using all things as though not using them, being deprived of all things, yet wanting nothing.

The divine action, being limitless in its fulness, can take possession of a soul only in as far as the soul is void of all confidence in her own action; for this confidence and self-activity fill the heart to the exclusion of the divine action. It is an obstacle which, existing in the soul herself, is more likely to arrest the divine action than exterior obstacles, which Providence can change at will into powerful aids; for it can work with all things, even those which are in themselves useless. With the divine will nothing is everything, and without it everything is nothing.

Whatever the value in itself of meditation, contemplation, vocal prayer, interior silence, acts of the will whether sensible, distinct, or less perceptible, retreat, or active life,—better than all of them is what God wills for the soul at the present moment; and the soul should regard everything else with perfect indifference, as being of no value whatever.

Thus seeing God alone in all things, she should take or leave them at His pleasure in order to live in, hope in, and be nourished by Him, and not by the things which have force and virtue only through Him. Under all circumstances the soul should constantly say with St. Paul, "Lord, what wouldst Thou have me do?" Not this more than that, but simply Thy adorable will! The spirit loves one thing, the flesh another; but, Lord, let Thy will be mine. Contemplation, action, prayer vocal or mental, affective or passive, light or darkness, special or general graces,—all these are nothing, Lord, for in Thy will lies their sole virtue. Thy will alone is the end of all my devotion, and not these things, however elevated or sublime in themselves; for the end of divine grace is the perfection of the heart, not of the mind.

The presence of God which sanctifies our souls is that indwelling of the Trinity which penetrates to the depths of our hearts when they are submissive to the divine will; for the presence of God which we enjoy through the exercise of contemplation effects this intimate union in us only as do all other things which come to us in the order of God. It holds, however, the first rank among them, for it is the most excellent means of uniting one's self with God when He wills that we should use it.

We may therefore justly esteem and love contemplation and other pious exercises, provided the foundation of this esteem and love be wholly God, who mercifully deigns through them to communicate Himself to our souls.

We receive the prince himself when we receive his suite. It would be showing him little respect to neglect his officers under pretext of possessing him alone.

CHAPTER VII.

There is no Enduring Peace but in Submission to the Divine Action.

The soul that is not united solely to the will of God will find neither rest nor sanctification in any self-chosen means—not even in the most excellent exercises of piety. If that which God Himself chooses for you does not suffice, what other hand can minister to your desires? If you turn from the food the divine will itself has prepared for you, what viands will not prove insipid to a taste so depraved? A soul cannot be truly nourished, strengthened, purified, enriched, sanctified, except by the fulness of the present moment. Then what more would you have? Since you here find all good, why seek it elsewhere? Are you wiser than God? Since He ordains it should be thus, how could you desire it should be otherwise? Can His wisdom and goodness err? Should you not from the moment He ordains an event be utterly convinced that it is the best that could happen? Do you think you will find peace in struggling with the Almighty? On the contrary, is it not this struggle too often renewed, almost unconsciously, which is the cause of all our disquiet. It is but just that the soul which is not satisfied with the divine fulness of the present moment should be punished by an inability to find contentment in anything else.

If books, the example of the saints, spiritual discourses, destroy the peace of the soul, if they fill without satisfying, it is a mark that we have not received them in simple abandonment to the divine action, but have taken them ourselves in a spirit of proprietorship. Their fulness, therefore, bars the entrance of God to the soul, and we must rid ourselves of it as an obstacle to grace. But when the divine action ordains the use of these means, the soul receives them as it does everything else—that is, in the order of God. She accepts them as she finds them, in her fidelity simply using them, never appropriating them; and their moment passed she abandons them to find her contentment in what follows in the order of Providence. In truth there is nothing really beneficial for me but that which comes to me in the order of God. Nowhere can I find any means, however good in itself, more efficacious for my sanctification and more capable of giving peace to my soul.

CHAPTER VIII.

The Perfection of Souls and the Excellence of Different States are in Proportion to their Conformity to the Order of God.

The order of God gives to all things which concern the faithful soul a supernatural and divine value; all that it exacts, all that it embraces, and all the objects upon which it sheds its light become holiness and perfection, for its virtue is limitless: it makes all that it touches divine. But in order to keep ourselves in the path of perfection, swerving neither to the right nor the left, the soul must follow no inspiration which she assumes comes from God without first assuring herself that it does not interfere with the duties of her state in life. These duties are the most certain indications of the will of God, and nothing should be preferred to them; in fulfilling them there is nothing to be feared, no exclusion or discrimination to be made; the moments devoted to them are the most precious and salutary for the soul from the fact that she is sure of accomplishing the good pleasure of God. All the perfection of the saints consists in their fidelity to the order of God; therefore we must refuse nothing, seek nothing, but accept all from His hand, and nothing without Him. Books, wise counsels, vocal prayers, interior affections, if they come to us in the order of God, instruct, guide, and unite the soul to Him. Quietism errs when it disclaims these means and all sensible appearances, for there are souls whom God wills shall be always led in this way, and their state and their attractions clearly indicate it. In vain we picture to ourselves methods of abandonment whence all action is excluded. When the order of God causes us to act, our sanctification lies in action.

Besides the duties of each one's state, God may further ask certain actions which are not included in these duties, though not contrary to them. Attraction and inspiration, then, indicate the divine order; and the most perfect for souls whom God leads in this way is to add to things of precept, things inspired, but always with the precautions which inspiration requires to prevent its interfering with the duties of one's state and the ordinary events of Providence.

God makes saints as He chooses. They are formed by His divine action, to which they are ever submissive, and this submission is the truest abandonment and the most perfect.

Fidelity to the duties of one's state and submission to the dispositions of Providence are common to all the saints. They live hidden in obscurity, for the world is so fatal to holiness that they would avoid its quicksands; but not in this does their sanctity consist, but wholly in their entire submission to the order of God. The more absolute their submission the greater their sanctity. We must not imagine that those whose virtues God is pleased to brilliantly manifest by singular and extraordinary works, by undoubted attractions and inspirations, are any less faithful in the path of abandonment. Once the order of God makes these brilliant works a duty they fail in abandonment to Him and His will which ceases to rule their every moment, and their every moment ceases to be the exponent of the will of God if they content themselves with the duties of their state and the ordinary events of Providence. They must study and measure their efforts according to the standard of God's designs for them in that path which their attractions indicate to them. Fidelity to inspiration is for them a duty; and as there are souls whose whole duty is marked by an exterior law, and who must be guided by it because God confines them to it, so also there are others who, besides their exterior duties, must be further faithful to that interior law which the Holy Spirit engraves upon their hearts.

But who are the most perfect? Vain and idle research! Each one must follow the path which is traced for him. Perfection consists in absolute submission to the order of God and carefully availing ourselves of all that is most perfect therein. It advances us little to weigh the advantages of the different states considered in themselves, since it is neither in the quality nor quantity of things enjoined that sanctity is to be sought. If self-love be the principle of our actions, or if we do not correct it when we recognize its workings, we will be always poor in the midst of an abundance not provided by the order of God. However, to decide in a measure the question, I think that sanctity corresponds to the love one has for God's good pleasure, and the greater one's love for this holy will and this order, whatever the character of their manifestations, the greater one's sanctity. This is manifest in Jesus, Mary, and Joseph, for in their private life there is more of love than of grandeur, and more of spirit than of matter; and it is not written that these sacred persons sought the holiest of things, but holiness in all things.

We must therefore conclude that there is no special way which can be called the most perfect, but that the most perfect in general is fidelity to the order of God, whether in the accomplishment of exterior duties or in the interior dispositions, each one according to his state and calling.

I believe that if souls seriously aspiring to perfection understood this, and knew how direct is their path, they would be spared much difficulty. I say the same equally of souls living in the world and of souls consecrated to God. If the first knew the means of merit afforded them by their ever-recurring daily duties and the ordinary actions of their state in life; if the second could persuade themselves that the foundation of sanctity lies in those very things which they consider unimportant and even foreign to them; if both could understand that the crosses sent by Providence which they constantly find in their state in life lead them to the highest perfection by a surer and shorter path than do extraordinary states or extraordinary works; and that the true philosopher's stone is submission to the order of God, which changes into pure gold all their occupations, all their weariness, all their sufferings—how happy they would be!

What consolation and what courage they would gather from this thought, that to acquire the friendship of God and all the glory of heaven they have but to do what they are doing, suffer what they are suffering; and that what they lose and count as naught would suffice to obtain them eminent sanctity. O my God, that I might be the missionary of Thy holy will, and teach the whole world that there is nothing so easy, so simple, so within the reach of all, as sanctity! Would that I could make them understand that just as the good and bad thief had the same to do and suffer to obtain their salvation, so two souls, one worldly and the other wholly interior and spiritual, have nothing more to do, one than the other; that she who sanctifies herself acquires eternal happiness by doing in submission to the will of God what she who is lost does through caprice; and that the latter is lost by suffering unwillingly and impatiently what she who is saved endures with resignation. The difference, therefore, is only in the heart.

O dear souls who read this, let me repeat to you: Sanctity will cost you no more; do what you are doing; suffer what you are suffering: it is only your heart that need be changed. By the heart we mean the will. This change, then, consists in willing what comes to us by the order of God. Yes, holiness of heart is a simple *fiat*, a simple disposition of conformity to the will of God. And what is easier? For who could not love so adorable and merciful a will? Let us love it, then, and through this love alone all within us will become divine.

CHAPTER IX.

All the Riches of Grace are the Fruit of Purity of Heart and Perfect Self-abandonment.

He, therefore, who would abundantly enjoy all good has but to purify his heart, detach himself from creatures, and completely abandon himself to the will of God. In this purity of heart and self-abandonment he will find all things.

Let others, Lord, ask Thee all gifts, let them multiply their petitions; I have but one gift to ask, but one prayer to make: Give me a pure heart. O blessed pure of heart! In thy lively faith thou beholdest God within thee. Thou seest Him in all things, and thou seest Him at all times working within thee and about thee. Thou art in all things His subject and His instrument. He guides thee in all things and leads thee to all things. Frequently thou art unmindful; but He thinks for thee. He only asks that thou *desire* all that comes to thee or may come to thee by His divine order. He *understands the preparation of thy heart.* In thy salutary blindness thou seekest in vain to discover this desire; but oh! it is clear to Him. How great is thy simplicity! Knowest thou not that a well-disposed heart is no other than a heart in which God dwells? Beholding His own desires in this heart He knows it will be ever submissive to His order. He knows at the same time that thou art ignorant what is best for thee, therefore it is His care to provide for thee. He cares not that thy designs are thwarted. Thou wouldst go east: He leads thee west. Thou art just upon the rocks: He turns the helm and brings thee safely into port. Though knowing neither chart, nor route, nor winds, nor tides, thy voyages are ever prosperous. If pirates cross thy way an unexpected breeze bears thee beyond their reach.

O good will! O purity of heart! Well did Jesus know your value when He placed ye among the beatitudes. What greater happiness than to possess God and be possessed by Him? O state most blessed and full of charm! In it we sleep peacefully in the bosom of Providence, sporting like a child with the divine wisdom, unheedful of our course, which is ever onward; in spite of shoals, and pirates, and continual storms, we are borne on to a prosperous end.

O purity of heart! O good will! Ye are the sole foundation of all spiritual states. To you are given, and through you are made profitable, the gifts of pure faith, pure hope, pure confidence, and pure love. Upon your stem are grafted the desert flowers—I mean those graces which we rarely find blooming but in utterly detached souls, of which God takes possession as of an uninhabited dwelling, and there abides to the exclusion of all other things. You are that bountiful source whence flow all the streams which water the parterre of the bridegroom and the garden of the bride. Alas! how truly mayest thou say to all souls: Consider me well; I am the mother of fair love—that love which develops all that is best and takes it to itself. It is I who give birth to that sweet and salutary fear which inspires a horror of evil, and makes you peacefully avoid it; I who ripen the sublime knowledge of God's greatness and reveal the value of the virtues which honor Him. It is I, finally, who inspire those ardent desires which, unceasingly sustained by holy confidence, stimulate you to practise virtue in the expectation of that divine object, the enjoyment of which will one day become, even as it is now (though then in a much more perfect degree), the happiness of faithful souls. Well mayest thou invite them all to enrich themselves from thy inexhaustible treasures, for thou art the source of all spiritual conditions and ways. From thee do they draw all their beauty, attraction, and charm. Those marvellous fruits of grace and virtue which dazzle us on all sides, and with which our devotion is nourished, are thy harvests. Thine is the land of abundance and honey; thy breasts distil milk, thy bosom gives out the sweet odor of myrrh; through thy fingers flow in all its purity the divine wine which usually must be obtained by the labor of the wine-press.

Let us fly then, dear souls, and plunge ourselves in that sea of love which invites us. What await we? Why do we tarry? Let us hasten to lose ourselves in God, in His very heart, that we may inebriate ourselves with the wine of His charity; in this heart we shall find the key to all heavenly treasures. Then let us proceed on our way to heaven, for there is no secret of perfection which we may not penetrate: every avenue is open to us, even to the garden, the cellar, the vineyard of the Bridegroom. If we would breathe the air of the fields we have but to direct our steps thither; in a word, we may come and go at will armed with this key of David, this key of knowledge, this key of the abyss which contains the hidden treasures of the divine wisdom. With it we may also open the gates of the mystic death and descend into its sacred shades; we may go down into the depths of the sea and into the den of the lion. It is this divine key which unlocks those dark dungeons into which it thrusts souls, to withdraw them purified and sanctified; it introduces us into those blissful abodes where light and knowledge dwell, where the Bridegroom takes His repose at midday, and where He reveals to His faithful souls the secrets of His love. O divine secrets, which may not be revealed, and which no mortal tongue can express! This key, dear souls, is love. All blessings wait only for love to enrich us. It gives sanctity and all its accompaniments; its right hand and its left are filled with it that it may pour it in abundance from all sources into hearts open to divine grace. O divine seed of eternity! who can sufficiently praise thee? But why seek to praise thee? It is better to possess thee in silence than to praise thee by feeble words. What am I saying? We must praise thee, but only because thou possessest us. For once thou possessest the heart, whether we read or write, or speak, or act, or are silent, it is all one and the same. We assume nothing, we refuse nothing; we are hermits, we are apostles; we are ill, we are well, we are simple, we are eloquent; in a word, we are what God wills we should be. The heart hears thy mandates, and, as thy faithful echo, repeats them to the other faculties. In this material and spiritual combination which thou deignest to regard as thy kingdom the heart governs under thy guidance; as it contains no desires uninspired by thee, all objects please it under whatever form thou presentest them. Those which nature or the Evil One would substitute for thine only fill it with disgust and horror. If sometimes thou permittest the heart to be surprised, it is only that it may become wiser and more humble; but as soon as it recognizes its illusion it returns to thee with more love, and binds itself to Thee with greater fidelity.

Book Second.
The Divine Action and the Manner in which it unceasingly works the Sanctification of Souls.

CHAPTER I.

The Divine Action is everywhere and always Present, though only Visible to the Eye of Faith.

All creatures are living in the hand of God; the senses perceive only the action of the creature, but faith sees the divine action in all things. Faith realizes that Jesus Christ lives in all things and works through all ages; that the least moment and the smallest atom contain a portion of this hidden life, this mysterious action. The instrumentality of creatures is a veil which covers the profound mysteries of the divine action. The apparition of Jesus to His Apostles after His resurrection surprised them: He presented Himself to them under forms which disguised Him, and as soon as He manifested Himself He disappeared. This same Jesus, who is ever living and laboring for us, still surprises souls whose faith is not sufficiently lively to discern Him.

There is no moment when God is not present with us under the appearance of some obligation or some duty. All that is effected within us, about us, and through us involves and hides His divine action: it is veritably present, though in an invisible manner; therefore we do not discern it, and only recognize its workings when it has ceased to act. Could we pierce the veil which obscures it, and were we vigilant and attentive, God would unceasingly reveal Himself to us, and we would recognize His action in all that befell us. At every event we would exclaim, *Dominus est!*—It is the Lord! and we should feel each circumstance of our life an especial gift from Him. We should regard creatures as feeble instruments in the hands of an all-powerful workman; we should easily recognize that we lacked nothing, and that God's watchful care supplied the needs of every moment. Had we faith, we should be grateful to all creatures; we should cherish them, and in our hearts thank them that in the hand of God they have been so serviceable to us and so favorable to the work of our perfection.

If we lived an uninterrupted life of faith we should be in continual communion with God, we should speak with Him face to face. Just as the air transmits our words and thoughts, so would all that we are called to do and suffer transmit to us the words and thoughts of God; all that came to us would be but the embodiment of His word; it would be exteriorly manifested in all things; we should find everything holy and profitable. The glory of God makes this the state of the blessed in heaven, and faith would make it ours on earth; there would be only the difference of means.

Faith is God's interpreter; without its enlightenment we understand nothing of the language of created things. It is a writing in cipher, in which we see naught but confusion; it is a burning bush, from the midst of which we little expect to hear God's voice. But faith reveals to us as to Moses the fire of divine charity burning in the midst of the bush; it gives the key to the ciphers, and discovers to us in the midst of the confusion the wonders of the divine wisdom. Faith gives to the whole earth a heavenly aspect; faith transports, enraptures the heart, and raises it above the things of this earth to converse with the blessed.

Faith is the light of time: it alone grasps the truth without seeing it; it touches what it does not feel; it sees this world as though it existed not, beholding quite other things than those which are visible. It is the key of the treasure-house, the key of the abyss, the key of the science of God. It is faith which shows the falseness of all creatures: through it God reveals and manifests Himself in all things; by it all things are made divine; it lifts the veil from created things and reveals the eternal truth.

All that our eyes behold is vanity and falsehood; in God alone lies the truth of all things. How far above our illusions are the designs of God! How is it that though continually reminded that all that passes in the world is but a shadow, a figure, a mystery of faith, we are guided by human feelings, by the natural sense of things, which after all is but an enigma? We foolishly fall into snares instead of lifting our eyes and rising to the principle, the source, the origin of all; where all things bear other names and other qualities; where all is supernatural, divine, sanctifying; where all is part of the fulness of Jesus Christ; where everything forms a stone of the heavenly Jerusalem, where everything leads to this marvellous edifice and enters therein. We live by the things of sight and hearing, neglecting that light of faith which would safely guide us through the labyrinth of shadows and images through which we foolishly wander. He, on the contrary, who walks by faith seeks but God alone, and all things from God; he lives in God; unheeding and rising above the figures of sense.

CHAPTER II.

The Divine Action is all the more Visible to the Eye of Faith when hidden under Appearances most Repugnant to the Senses.

The soul enlightened by faith is far from judging of created things, like those who measure them by their senses, and ignore the inestimable treasure they contain. He who recognizes the king in disguise treats him very differently from him who, judging by appearances alone, fails to recognize his royalty. So the soul that sees the will of God in the smallest things, and in the most desolating and fatal events, receives all with equal joy, exultation, and respect. That which others fear and fly from with horror she opens all her doors to receive with honor. The retinue is poor, the senses despise it; but the heart, under these humble appearances, discerns and does homage to the royal majesty; and the more this majesty abases itself, coming secretly with modest suite, the deeper is the love it inspires in the heart.

I have no words with which to portray the feelings of the heart when it receives this divine will in the guise of humiliation, poverty, annihilation. Ah! how moved was the beautiful heart of Mary at sight of that poverty of a God, that annihilation which brought Him to lodge in a manger, to repose on a handful of straw a trembling, weeping infant! Ask the people of Bethlehem what they think of this child: were He in a palace with royal surroundings they would do Him homage. But ask Mary, Joseph, the Magi, the shepherds: they will tell you that in this extreme poverty they find that which manifests God to them more sublime and adorable. By just that which the senses lack is faith heightened, increased, and nourished; the less there is to human eyes, the more there is to the soul. The faith which adores Jesus on Thabor, which loves the will of God in extraordinary events, is not that lively faith which loves the will of God in common events and adores Jesus on the cross. For the perfection of faith is seen only when visible and material things contradict it and seek to destroy it. Through this war of the senses faith comes out gloriously victorious.

It is not an ordinary but a grand and extraordinary faith which finds God equally adorable in the simplest and commonest things as in the greatest events of life.

To content ones' self with the present moment is to love and adore the divine will in all that comes to us to do or suffer through the things which successively form the duties of the present moment. Souls thus disposed adore God with redoubled ardor and respect in the greatest humiliations; nothing hides Him from the piercing eye of their faith. The more vehemently the senses exclaim, This is not from God! the closer do they press this bundle of myrrh from the hand of the Bridegroom; nothing disturbs them, nothing repels them.

Mary sees the Apostles fly, but she remains constant at the foot of the cross; she recognizes her Son in that face spat upon and bruised. These disfiguring wounds only render Him more adorable and worthy of love in the eyes of this tender mother; and the blasphemies poured forth against Him only serve to increase her profound veneration. In like manner, a life of faith is but a continual pursuit of God through all which disguises and disfigures Him; through all which, so to speak, destroys and annihilates Him. It is truly a reproduction of the life of Mary, who from the manger to Calvary remained constant to a God whom the world despised, persecuted, and abandoned. So faithful souls, despite a continual succession of deaths, veils, shadows, semblances which disguise the will of God, perseveringly pursue it, and love it unto death on the cross. They know that, unheeding all disguises, they must follow this holy will; for, beyond the heaviest shadows, beyond the darkest clouds, the divine Sun is shining to enlighten, enflame, and vivify those constant hearts who bless, praise, and contemplate Him from all points of this mysterious horizon.

Hasten, then, happy, faithful, untiring souls; hasten to follow this dear Spouse who with giant strides traverses the heavens and from whom nothing can be hidden. He passes over the smallest blade of grass as above the loftiest cedars. The grains of sand are under His feet no less than the mountains. Wherever your foot may rest He has passed, and you have only to follow Him faithfully to find Him wherever you go.

Oh, the ineffable peace that is ours when faith has taught us thus to see God through all creatures as through a transparent veil! Then darkness becomes light, and bitter turns to sweet. Faith, manifesting all things in their true light, changes their deformity into beauty, and their malice into virtue. Faith is the mother of meekness, confidence, and joy; she can feel naught but tenderness and compassion for her enemies who so abundantly enrich her at their own expense. The more malignant the action of the creature, the more profitable does God render it to the soul. While the human instrument seeks to injure us, the divine Artisan in whose hand it lies makes use of its very malice to remove what is prejudicial to the soul.

The will of God has only consolations, graces, treasures, for submissive souls; our confidence in it cannot be too great, nor our abandonment thereto be too absolute. It always wills and effects that which contributes most to our sanctification, provided meanwhile we yield ourselves to its divine action. Faith never doubts it; the more unbelieving, rebellious, despondent, and wavering the senses, the louder Faith cries, "This is God! All is well!"

There is nothing Faith does not penetrate and overcome; it passes beyond all shadows and through the darkest clouds to reach Truth; clasps it in a firm embrace, and is never parted from it.

CHAPTER III.

The Divine Action offers us at each Moment Infinite Blessings, which we receive in proportion to our Faith and Love.

If we knew how to greet each moment as the manifestation of the divine will, we would find in it all the heart could desire. For what indeed is more reasonable, more perfect, more divine than the will of God? Can its infinite value be increased by the paltry difference of time, place, or circumstance? Were you given the secret of finding it at all times and in all places, you would possess a gift most precious, most worthy of your desires. What seek ye, holy souls? Give free scope to your longings; place no limit to your aspirations; expand your heart to the measure of the infinite. I have that wherewith to satisfy it: there is no moment in which I may not cause you to find all you can desire.

The present moment is always filled with infinite treasures: it contains more than you are capable of receiving. Faith is the measure of these blessings: in proportion to your faith will you receive. By love also are they measured: the more your heart loves the more it desires, and the more it desires the more it receives. The will of God is constantly before you as an unfathomable sea, which the heart cannot exhaust: only in proportion as the heart is expanded by faith, confidence, and love can it receive of its fulness. All created things could not fill your heart, for its capacity is greater than anything which is not God.

The mountains which affright the eye are but atoms to the heart. The divine will is an abyss, of which the present moment is the entrance; plunge fearlessly therein and you will find it more boundless than your desires. Offer no homage to creatures; adore not phantoms: they can give you nothing, they can take nothing from you. The will of God alone shall be your fulness, and it shall leave no void in your soul. Adore it; go direct to it, penetrating all appearances, casting aside all impediments. The spoliation, the destruction, the death of the senses is the reign of faith. The senses adore creatures; faith adores the divine will. Wrest from the senses their idols, they will weep like disconsolate children; but faith will triumph, for nothing can take from her the will of God. When all the senses are famished, affrighted, despoiled, then does the will of God nourish, enrich, and fortify faith, which smiles at these apparent losses, as the commander of an impregnable fortress smiles at the futile attacks of an enemy.

When the will of God reveals itself to a soul manifesting a desire to wholly possess her, if the soul freely give herself in return she experiences most powerful assistance in all difficulties; she then tastes by experience the happiness of that coming of the Lord, and her enjoyment is in proportion to the degree in which she learned to practise that self abandonment which must bring her at all moments face to face with this ever adorable will.

CHAPTER IV.

God reveals Himself to us as Mysteriously, as Adorably, and with as much Reality in the most Ordinary Events as in the great Events of History and the Holy Scriptures.

The written word of God is full of mystery; His word expressed in the events of the world is no less so. These two books are truly sealed; the letter of both killeth.

God is the centre of faith which is an abyss from whose depths shadows rise which encompass all that comes forth from it. God is incomprehensible; so also are His works, which require our faith. All these words, all these works, are but obscure rays, so to speak, of a sun still more obscure. In vain do we strive to gaze upon this sun and its rays with the eyes of our body; the eyes of the soul itself, through which we behold God and His works, are no less closed. Obscurity here takes the place of light; knowledge is ignorance, and we see though not seeing. Holy Scripture is the mysterious language of a still more mysterious God. The events of the world are the mysterious utterances of this same hidden and inscrutable God. They are drops of the ocean, but an ocean of shadows. Every rivulet, every drop of the stream, bears the impress of its origin. The fall of the angels, the fall of man, the wickedness and idolatry of men before and after the deluge, in the time of the Patriarchs who knew the history of creation, with its recent preservation, and related it to their children,—these are the truly mysterious words of Holy Scripture. A handful of men preserved from idolatry amid the general corruption of the whole world until the coming of the Messias; evil always dominant, always powerful; the little band of the defenders of the faith always ill-treated, always persecuted; the persecution of Christ; the plagues of the Apocalypse—in these behold the words of God.

It is what He has revealed. It is what He has dictated. And the effects of these terrible mysteries, which endure till the end of time, are still the living words of God by which we learn His wisdom, goodness, and power. All the events in the history of the world show forth these attributes and glorify Him therein. We must believe it blindly, for, alas! we cannot see.

What does God teach us by Turks, heretics, and all the enemies of His Church? They preach forcibly. They all show forth His infinite perfections. So do Pharao and all the impious hosts who followed him and will still follow him; though truly, to the evidence of our senses, the end of all these is most contrary to the divine glory. We must close our corporal eyes and cease to reason if we would read the divine mysteries in all this.

Thou speakest, Lord, to all mankind by general events. All revolutions are but the tides of Thy Providence, which excite storms and tempests in the minds of the curious. Thou speakest to each one in particular by the events of his every moment. But instead of respecting the mystery and obscurity of Thy words, and hearing Thy voice in all the occurrences of life, they only see therein chance, the acts, the caprice of men; they find fault in everything; they would add to, diminish, reform—in fact, they indulge in liberties with these living words of God, while they would consider it a sacrilege to alter a comma of the Holy Scriptures. The Scriptures they revere: they are the word of God, they tell you; they are true and holy. Though they may comprehend them little, their veneration for them is no less great, and they justly give honor and glory to God for the depth of His wisdom.

But, dear souls, have you no respect for the words God addresses you each moment,—words which are not conveyed to you by means of ink and paper, but by what you have to do and suffer from moment to moment,—do these words merit nothing from you? Why do you not revere the truth and will of God in all things? There is nothing which fully satisfies you; you criticise and cavil at all that happens. Do you not see that you try to measure by the senses and reason that which can be measured by faith alone? And that while reading the word of God in the Holy Scriptures with the eyes of faith, you gravely err when you read this same word with other eyes in His works?

CHAPTER V.

The Divine Action continues in our Hearts the Revelation begun in Holy Scripture; but the Characters in which it is written will be Visible only at the Last Day.

"Jesus Christ," says the Apostle, "is the same yesterday, to-day, and forever." From the beginning of the world He was, as God, the principle of the life of just souls. From the first moment of His incarnation His humanity shared this prerogative of His divinity. Throughout our whole lives He is working within us. The time of this world is but a day, and this day is full of Him. Jesus Christ lived, and He still lives. He began in Himself, and He continues in His saints, a life which will never end. O life of Jesus, which embraces and exceeds all ages! Life which unceasingly worketh new wonders! If the world is incapable of embracing all that could have been written of the actual life of Jesus, of all that He said and did upon earth; if the Gospel gives us only a few traits of it; if so little is known even of that first hidden yet fruitful hour of Bethlehem,—how many gospels must needs be written to relate all the moments of that mystic life of Jesus Christ which multiplies wonders infinitely, multiplies them eternally!—for all times, properly speaking, are but the history of the divine action.

The Holy Spirit has marked in infallible and incontestable characters certain moments of this vast duration, and gathered in the Scriptures some drops of this boundless ocean. We see therein the secret and hidden ways by which He has manifested Jesus Christ to the world. We can follow the channels and veins which, amid the confusion of the children of men, distinguish this Firstborn. The Old Testament is but a small portion of the innumerable and inscrutable ways of this divine work; it only contains what is necessary to reach Jesus Christ. The Holy

Spirit held the rest hidden in the treasures of His wisdom. And from out this vast sea of the divine action but a thread of water appears which reaches Jesus, loses itself in the Apostles, and is swallowed up in the Apocalypse. So that by our faith alone can we learn the history of this divine action which consists in the life which Jesus Christ leads, and will lead in just souls until the end of time.

To the manifestation of God's truth by word succeeded the manifestation of His charity by action. The Holy Spirit continues the work of the Saviour. While He assists the Church in preaching the gospel of Christ, He Himself at the same time writes His own gospel in our hearts. Each moment, each act, of the Saints is the gospel of the Holy Spirit. Holy souls are the paper; their sufferings, their actions, are the ink. The Holy Spirit by the pen of His action writes a living gospel; but we can only read it on the last day, when it will be drawn from the press of this life and published.

Oh, the glorious history, the beautiful book, which the Holy Spirit is now writing! It is in press, holy souls; and not a day passes in which type is not set, ink applied, and sheets of it printed. But we are in the night of faith: the paper is blacker than the ink; the characters are confused; it is the language of another world; we understand it not; we shall only read its gospel in heaven. Oh, if we could but see this life of God in all creatures, in all things, and learn to regard them, not in themselves, but as the instruments of His will! If we could see how the divine action impels them hither and thither, unites them, disperses them, opposes them, and leads them by contrary ways to the same end, we should recognize that all things have their purpose, their reason, their proportion, their relations in this divine work. But how shall we read this book with its hidden, innumerable, contradictory, and obscure characters? If the combinations of twenty-seven letters are incomprehensible to us and suffice to form an unlimited number of different volumes, each admirable of its kind, who can express what God does in His universe? Who can read and comprehend a book so vast, in which there is not a letter which has not its own significance and does not contain in its littleness profound mysteries? Mysteries are neither seen nor felt; they are the subjects of faith. Faith judges their worth and truth only by their source, for they are so obscure in themselves that all their external appearances only serve to conceal them, and mislead those who judge by reason alone.

Teach me, O divine Spirit, to read in this book of life! I would become Thy disciple, and like a little child believe what I cannot see. It sufficeth that my Master speaks. He tells me this, He proclaims that; His words are arranged in one form. He interprets them in another: that sufficeth me; I receive all as He presents it; I see not the reason thereof, but I know He is the infallible Truth. His words, His actions, are truth. He wills that these letters should form a word; such a number, another. They are but three, but six; yet no more are required, and less would mar the sense. He alone who knows all thought can combine the characters to express it. Everything is significant; everything has a perfect meaning. This line purposely ends here; there is not a comma lacking therein, nor one useless point. I believe it now; but on that glorious day, when so many mysteries will be revealed me, I will see what I now only confusedly comprehend; and that which appears so obscure, so perplexing, so contradictory to reason, so vague, so visionary, will enrapture and delight me to all eternity with the beauty, the order, the meaning, the wisdom, and the inconceivable marvels I shall discover therein.

CHAPTER VI.

Divine Love is communicated to us through the Veil of Creatures, as Jesus communicates Himself to us through the Veil of the Eucharistic Species.

What sublime truths are hidden even from Christians who believe themselves most enlightened! How many are there who realize that every cross, every action, every attraction in the order of God gives Him to us in a manner which cannot be better explained than by comparison with the august mystery of the Eucharist! Yet what is more certain? Does not reason, as well as faith, reveal to us the real presence of divine love in all creatures, in all the events of life, as infallibly as the word of Christ and His Church reveal to us the presence of the sacred Body of the Saviour under the Eucharistic species? Do we not know that the divine love seeks to communicate itself to us through all creatures and through all events?—that it has effected, ordered, or permitted all our surroundings, all that befalls us, only in view of this union which is the sole end of all God's designs?—that for this end He makes use of the worst as well as the best creatures, of the most grievous as well as the most pleasing events?—and that our union with Him is even the more meritorious that the means which serve to make the union closer are of a nature repugnant to us? But if all this be true, why should not each moment be a form of communion in which we receive divine love; and why should not this communion of every moment be as profitable to our souls as that in which we receive the Body and Blood of the Son of God? This latter, it is true, possesses sacramental grace, which the other does not; but, on the other hand, how much more frequently may not this first form of communion be repeated, and how greatly may its merit be increased, by the perfection of the dispositions with which it is accomplished! Therefore how true it is that the holiest life is mysterious in its simplicity and apparent lowliness! O heavenly

~ 53 ~

banquet! O never-ending feast! A God always given, and always received; not in sublime splendor or glorious light, but in utter infirmity, weakness, and nothingness! That which the natural man condemns, and human reason rejects, God chooses, and makes thereof mysteries, sacraments of love, giving Himself to souls through that which would seem to injure them most, and in proportion to their faith which finds Him in all things.

CHAPTER VII.

The Divine Action, the Will of God, is as unworthily treated and disregarded in its Daily Manifestation by many Christians as was Jesus in the Flesh by the Jews.

What infidelity we find in the world! How unworthily men think of God! They criticise His divine action as they would not dare to criticise the work of the humblest artisan. They would force Him to act within the narrow limits of their weak reason and follow its rules. They pretend to reform all things. They unceasingly complain and murmur.

They are shocked at the treatment Jesus received at the hands of the Jews. Ah! Divine Love! Adorable Will! Infallible Action! How do they look upon Thee? Can the divine will err? Can anything it sends be amiss? But I have this to do; I need such a thing; I have been deprived of the necessary means; that man thwarts me in such good works; is not this most unreasonable?—this sickness overtakes me when I absolutely need my health. No, dear souls, the will of God is all that is absolutely necessary to you, therefore you do not need what He withholds from you—you lack nothing. If you could read aright these things which you call accidents, disappointments, misfortunes, contradictions, which you find unreasonable, untimely, you would blush with confusion; you would regard your murmurs as blasphemies: but you do not reflect that all these things are simply the will of God. This adorable will is blasphemed by His dear children who fail to recognize it.

When Thou wert upon earth, O my Jesus! the Jews treated Thee as a sorcerer, called Thee a Samaritan; and now that Thou livest in all ages, how do we regard Thy adorable will forever worthy of praise and blessing? Has there been a moment from the creation to this present one in which we live, and will there be one to the last day, in which the holy Name of God is not worthy of praise?—that Name which fills all time, and all the events of time; that Name which renders all things salutary!

What! Can that which is called the will of God work me harm? Shall I fear, shall I fly from the will of God? Ah! where shall I go to find something more profitable if I fear the divine action and resist the effect of the divine will?

How faithfully we should listen to the words which are each moment uttered in the depths of our hearts! If our senses, our reason, hear not, penetrate not the truth and wisdom of these words, is it not because of their incapacity to divine eternal truths? Should I be surprised that a mystery disconcerts reason? God speaks; it is a mystery; therefore it is death to the senses and reason, for it is the nature of mysteries to immolate to themselves sense and reason. Through faith mystery becomes the life of the heart, to all else it is contradiction. The divine action killeth while it quickeneth; the more we feel death the firmer our faith that it will give life; the more obscure the mystery, the more light it contains. Hence it is that the simple soul finds nothing more divine than that which is least so externally. The life of faith wholly consists in this constant struggle against the senses.

CHAPTER VIII.

The Revelation of the Present Moment is the more Profitable that it is addressed Directly to us.

We are only truly instructed by the words which God pronounces expressly for us. It is neither by books nor curious research that we become learned in the science of God: these means of themselves give us but a vain knowledge, which only serves to confuse us and inflate us with pride.

That which really instructs us is all that comes to us by the order of God from one moment to another: this is the knowledge of experience, which Christ Himself was pleased to acquire before teaching. It was indeed the only knowledge in which, according to the words of the Gospel, He could grow; for as God there was no degree of speculative knowledge which He did not possess. But if this knowledge was needful to the Incarnate Word Himself, it is absolutely necessary for us if we would speak to the hearts of those whom God sends to us.

We only know perfectly that which we have learned by experience through suffering and action. This is the school of the Holy Spirit, who utters the words of life to the heart; and all that we say to others should come from this source. Whatsoever we read, whatsoever we see, becomes divine science only through the fecundity, the virtue, the light, which the possession of this experience gives. Without this science all our learning is like unleavened dough, lacking the salt and seasoning of experience; the mind is filled with crude, unfledged ideas; and we are like the dreamer who, knowing all the highways of the world, misses the path to his own home.

Therefore we have only to listen to God's voice from moment to moment if we would learn the science of the saints, which is all practice and experience.

Heed not what is said to others; listen only to what is uttered for you and to you: you will find therein sufficient to exercise your faith, for this hidden language of God by its very obscurity exercises, purifies, and increases your faith.

CHAPTER IX.

The Revelation of the Present Moment is an Inexhaustible Source of Sanctity.

O all ye who thirst! know that you have not far to seek for the fountain of living waters; it springs close to you in the present moment. Hasten then to approach it. Why with the source so near do you weary yourselves running after shallow streams, which only excite your thirst and give you to drink in small measure? The source alone can satisfy you; it is inexhaustible. If you would think, write, and live like the Prophets, Apostles, and Saints, abandon yourself, like them, to divine inspiration.

O Love too little known! Men think Thy marvels are o'er, and that we have but to copy Thy ancient works and quote Thy former teachings! And they see not that Thy inexhaustible action is an infinite source of new thoughts, new sufferings, new works, new Patriarchs, new Prophets, new Apostles, new Saints, who have no need to copy the life or writings one of the other, but only to live in perpetual self-abandonment to Thy secret operations. We are wont to quote the "first ages of the Church!—the times of the saints!" But is not all time the effects of the divine action, the workings of the divine will, which absorbs all moments, fills them, sanctifies them, supernaturalizes them? Has there ever been a method of self-abandonment to the divine will which is not now practicable? From the earliest ages had the saints other secrets of holiness than that of becoming from moment to moment what the divine action would make them? And will not this action even to the end of time continue to pour its grace upon those who abandon themselves to it without reserve?

Rev. J. P. de Caussade

Yes, adorable, eternal Love! Love eternally fruitful and always marvellous! Will of my God, Thou art my book, my doctrine, my science; in Thee are my thoughts, my words, my deeds, my crosses. Not by consulting Thy other works can I become what Thou wouldst make me, but only by receiving Thee through all things in that one royal way of self-abandonment to Thy will—that ancient way, that way of my fathers. I will think, speak, and be enlightened like them; following in this way, I will imitate them, quote them, copy them, in all things.

CHAPTER X.

The Present Moment is the Manifestation of the Name of God and the Coming of His Kingdom.

The present moment is like an ambassador which declares the will of God. The heart must ever answer *fiat*, and the soul will go steadily on by means of all things to her centre and her term—never pausing in her course, spreading her sails to all winds; all ways, all methods equally further her progress towards the great, the infinite. All things afford her equal means of sanctification. The one only essential the soul finds in the present moment. It is no longer either prayer or silence, retirement or conversation, reading or writing, reflections or cessation of thought, avoidance or seeking of spiritualities, abundance or privation, illness or health, life or death, but simply what comes to her each moment by the order of God. In this consists that privation, abnegation, renouncement of created things, whether real or in will, in order that a soul may be nothing of herself or for herself, but live wholly by the order of God, and at His good pleasure content herself with the duty of the present moment, as though it were the one thing in the world.

If whatsoever comes to a soul thus self-abandoned is her one essential, we see clearly that she lacks nothing, and therefore should never complain; that if she murmur she lacks faith, and lives by reason and the senses alone, which, failing to recognize this sufficiency of grace, are ever discontented.

To bless the name of God according to the expression of the Scriptures is to love Him, adore Him, and recognize His holiness in all things. In fact, all things like words proceed from the mouth of God. The events of each moment are divine thoughts expressed by created objects; thus all things which intimate His will to us are so many names, so many words, by which He manifests His desires. This will is one in itself; it bears but one incomprehensible, ineffable name; but it is multiplied infinitely in its effects, and assumes their names. To sanctify the name of God is to study, adore, and love the ineffable Being whom this name represents. It is also to study, adore, and love His blessed will at all times, in all its effects; regarding all things as so many veils, shadows, names of this eternally holy will. It is holy in all its works, holy in all its words, holy in all its forms of manifestation, holy in all the names it bears.

It was thus Job blessed the name of God. The holy man blessed his terrible desolation which expressed the will of God: he called it not ruin, but a name of the Lord; and blessing it he declared that this divine will expressed by the most terrible afflictions was ever holy, whatever form, whatever name it bore. David also blessed it at all times and in all places. Therefore it is by this continual manifestation, this revelation of the will of God in all things that His kingdom is within us that His will is done upon earth as it is in heaven, that He gives us our daily bread.

Abandonment to the divine will contains the substance of that incomparable prayer which Christ Himself has taught us. We repeat it vocally many times a day according to the order of God and His holy Church; but we utter it in the depth of our hearts each moment that we lovingly receive or suffer whatever is ordained by this adorable will. What the lips need words and time to express, the heart effectively utters with each pulsation, and thus simple souls unceasingly bless Him in the depth of their hearts. They sigh nevertheless over their inability to praise Him as they desire: so true it is that God gives His graces and favors to such souls by the very means which seem to deprive them of these blessings. This is the secret of the divine wisdom—to impoverish the senses while it enriches the heart, and to fill the heart in proportion to the aching void in the senses.

Let us learn then to recognize in the event of each moment the imprint of the will of God, of His adorable name. This name is infinitely holy. It is but just therefore to bless it and receive it as a form of sacrament which by its own virtue sanctifies the souls in which it finds no obstacle to its grace. Can we do other than infinitely esteem that which bears this august name? It is a divine manna which falls from heaven to continually strengthen us in grace. It is a kingdom of holiness which is established in the soul. It is the bread of angels which is given upon earth as it is in heaven. No moment can be unimportant since they all contain treasures of grace, angelic food.

Yes, Lord, let Thy kingdom come to my heart to sanctify it, to nourish it, to purify it, to render it victorious over my enemies. Precious moment! how insignificant thou art to the eyes of the world, but how grand to the eyes enlightened by faith! And can I call that little which is great in the eyes of my Father who reigns in heaven? All that comes thence is most excellent. All that descends therefrom bears the impress of its origin.

CHAPTER XI.

The Divine Will imparts the Highest Sanctity to Souls; they have but to abandon Themselves to its Divine Action.

It is only because they know not how to profit by the divine action that so many Christians spend their lives anxiously seeking hither and thither a multitude of means of sanctification; these are profitable when the divine will ordains them, but become injurious the moment they prevent one from simply uniting himself with the will of God. These multiplied means cannot give what we will find in the will of God—that principle of all life, which is ever present with us, and which imparts to its every instrument an original and incomparable action.

Jesus has sent us a master whom we do not heed. He speaks to all hearts, and to each one he utters the word of life, the incomparable word; but we hear it not. We would know what he says to others, and we hearken not to what is said to us. We do not sufficiently regard things in the supernatural light which the divine action gives them. We must always receive and worthily meet the divine action with an open heart, full confidence and generosity; for to those who thus receive it it can work no ill. This illimitable action, which from the beginning to the end of all ages is ever the same in itself, flows on through all moments, and gives itself in its immensity and its virtue to the simple soul which adores it, loves it, and solely rejoices in it. You would be enraptured, you say, to find an occasion of sacrificing your life for God; such heroism enchants you. To lose all, to die forsaken and alone, to sacrifice one's self for others—such are the glorious deeds which enchant you.

But let me, O Lord, render glory, all glory, to Thy divine action! In it I find the happiness of the martyrs, austerities and sacrifice of self for others. This action, this will, sufficeth me. Whatever life or death it ordains for me I am content. It pleases me in itself far more than all its instruments and its effects, since it permeates all things, renders them divine, and transforms them into itself. It maketh heaven for me everywhere; all my moments are purely filled with the divine action; and living or dying, it is my sole contentment.

Yes, my Beloved, I will cease to prescribe Thee hours or methods; Thou shalt be ever welcome. O divine action, Thou seemest to have revealed me Thy immensity. I will but walk henceforth in the bosom of Thy infinity. The tide of Thy power flows to-day as it flowed yesterday. Thy foundation is the bed of the torrent whence graces unceasingly flow; Thou holdest the waters thereof in Thy hand, and movest them at will. No longer will I seek Thee within the narrow limits of a book, the life of a saint, a sublime thought. No: these are but drops of that great ocean which embraces all creatures. The divine action inundates them all. They are but atoms which sink into this abyss. No longer will I seek this action in spiritual intercourse. No more will I beg my bread from door to door. I will depend upon no creature.

Yes, Lord, I would live to Thy honor as the worthy child of a true Father, infinitely good, wise, and powerful. I would live as I believe, and since the divine action labors incessantly and by means of all things for my sanctification, I would draw my life from this great and boundless reservoir, ever present, and ever practically available. Is there a creature whose action equals that of God? And since this uncreated hand directs all that comes to me, shall I go in search of aid from creatures who are impotent, ignorant, and indifferent to me? I was dying of thirst; I ran from fountain to fountain, from stream to stream; and behold at hand was a source which caused a deluge; water surrounded me on all sides! Yes, everything becomes bread to nourish me, water to cleanse me, fire to purify me, a chisel to give me celestial form. Everything is an instrument of grace for my necessities; that which I sought in other things seeks me incessantly and gives itself to me by means of all creatures.

O Love! will men never see that Thou meetest them at every step, while they seek Thee hither and thither, where Thou art not? When in the open country, what folly not to breathe its pure air; to pause and study my steps when the path is smooth before me; to thirst when the flood encompasses me; to hunger for God when I may find Him, relish Him, and receive His will through all things!

Seek you, dear souls, the secret of union with God? There is none other than to avail yourselves of all that He sends you. All things may further this union; all things perfect it, save sin, and that which is contrary to your duty. You have but to accept all that He sends and let it do its work in you.

Everything is a banner to guide you, a stay to uphold you, an easy and safe vehicle to bear you on.

Everything is the hand of God. Everything is earth, air, and water to the soul. God's action is more universally present than the elements. His grace penetrates you through all your senses provided you but use them according to His order; for you must guard and close them to all that is not His will. There is not an atom which, entering your frame, may not cause this divine action to penetrate to the very marrow of your bones. It is the source and origin of all things. The vital fluid which flows in your veins moves only by order of the divine will; all the variations of your system, strength or weakness, languor or vigor, life or death, are but the instruments with which the divine action effects your sanctification. Under its influence all physical conditions become operations of grace. All your thoughts, all your emotions, whatever their apparent source, proceed from this invisible hand. No created mind or heart can teach you what this divine action will do in you; you will learn it by successive experience. Your life unceasingly flows into this incomprehensible abyss, where we have but to love and accept as best that which the present moment brings, with perfect confidence in this divine action which of itself can only work you good.

Yes, my Beloved, all souls might attain supernatural, admirable, inconceivably sublime states if they would but submit themselves to Thy divine action! Yes, if they would but yield to this divine hand they would attain eminent sanctity. All could reach it, since it is offered to all. You have but to open your heart and it will enter of itself: for there is no soul which does not possess in Thee, my God, its infinitely perfect model; no soul in which Thy divine action labors not unceasingly to render it like unto Thy image. If they were faithful they would all live, act, speak divinely; they need only copy one another; the divine action would signalize each one of them through the most ordinary things.

How, O my God! can I cause Thy creatures to relish what I advance? Must I, possessing a treasure capable of enriching all, see souls perish in their poverty? Must I see them die like desert plants when I point out to them the source of living waters? Come, simple souls, who have no feeling of devotion whatever, no talent, not even the first elements of instruction,—you who understand nothing of spiritual terms, who are filled with admiration and astonishment by the eloquence of the learned,—come and I will teach you the secret of excelling these brilliant intellects; and I will make perfection so attainable that you will find it within you, about you, around you, at every step. I will unite you to God, and He will hold you by the hand from the moment you begin to practise what I tell you. Come, not to learn the chart of this spiritual country, but to possess it, and to walk at ease therein without fear of going astray. Come, not to study the theory of divine grace, nor to learn what it has effected in all ages and is still effecting, but to be simply the subjects of its operations. You have no need to learn and ingenuously repeat the words addressed to others: divine grace shall utter to you alone all that you require.

CHAPTER XII.

The Divine Action alone can sanctify us, for it forms us after the Divine Model of our Perfection.

The divine action executes in time the designs of the eternal Wisdom in regard to all things. God alone can make known to each soul the design which it is destined to realize. Though you read the will of God in regard to others, this knowledge cannot direct you in anything. In the Word, in God Himself, is the design after which you should be formed, and after which you are modelled by the divine action. In the Word the divine action finds that to which every soul may be conformed. Holy Scripture contains a portion of this design, and the work of the Holy Spirit in souls completes it after the model which the Word presents. Is it not evident that the only secret for receiving the impress of this eternal design is to be passively submissive in His hands, and that no intellectual effort or speculation will help us to attain it? Is it not manifest that skill, intelligence, or subtlety of mind will not effect this work, but passive self-abandonment to the divine will, yielding ourselves like metal to the mould, like canvas to the brush, or like stone to the sculptor? It is clear that a knowledge of the divine mysteries which the will of God effects in all ages is not what renders us conformable to the design which the Word has conceived for us. No: it is the impress of the divine Hand; and this imprint is not graven in the mind through the medium of thought, but upon the will through its submission to the will of God.

The wisdom of the simple soul consists in contentment with what is suitable to her, in confining herself to the sphere of her duties, and in never going beyond its boundary. She is not curious to know the secrets of the divine economy: she is content with God's will in her regard, never striving to decipher its hidden meaning by conjecture or comparison, desiring to know no more than each moment reveals, listening to the voice of the Word when it speaks in the depth of her heart, never asking what the Spouse of her soul utters to others, contenting herself with what she receives in the depth of her soul; so that from moment to moment all things, however insignificant or whatever their nature, sanctify her unconsciously to herself. Thus the Beloved speaks to His spouse by the palpable effects of His action, which the spouse does not curiously study, but accepts with loving gratitude. Therefore the spirituality of this soul is simple, most solid, and interwoven with her whole being. Neither tumultuous thoughts nor words influence her conduct; for these, when not the instruments of divine grace, only inflate the mind. Many there are who assign an important part to intellect in piety, yet it is of little account therein, and not unfrequently prejudicial. We must make use of that only which God sends us to do and suffer. Yet many of us leave this divine essential to occupy our minds with the historic wonders of the divine work, instead of increasing these wonders by our fidelity.

The marvels of this work which gratify the curiosity of our readings serve only to disgust us with the apparently unimportant events through which, if we despise them not, the divine love effects great things in us. Foolish creatures that we are! We admire, we bless, this divine action in its written history; but when it would continue to write its gospel in our hearts, we hold the paper in continual unrest, and we impede its action by our curiosity to know what it effects in us and what it effects elsewhere.

Pardon, divine Love, for I am writing my own defects, and I have not yet learned what it is to abandon myself to Thy hand. I have not yet yielded myself to the mould. I have walked through Thy divine studios, I have admired all Thy works, but I have not yet learned the needful self-abandonment to receive the marks of Thy pencil. At last I have found Thee, my dear Master, my Teacher, my Father, my dear Love! I will be Thy disciple; I will learn in no other school but Thine. I return like the prodigal hungering for Thy bread. I abandon the ideas which only serve to gratify my curiosity. I will no longer seek after masters or books; no, I will use these means only as Thy divine will ordains them, and then not for my gratification, but to obey Thee by accepting all that Thou sendest me. I would confine myself solely to the duty of the present moment in order to prove my love, fulfil my obligations, and leave thee free to do with me what Thou wilt.

Book Third.
The Paternal Care with which God surrounds Souls wholly abandoned to Him.

CHAPTER I.

God Himself guides Souls who wholly abandon themselves to Him.

Sacrificate sacrificium justitiæ et sperate in Domino: Sacrifice, saith the prophet, a sacrifice of justice and hope in the Lord. That is to say that the grand and solid foundation of the spiritual life is to give one's self to God to be the subject of His good pleasure in all things, interiorly as well as exteriorly, and to so utterly forget self that we regard it as a thing sold and delivered, to which we have no longer any right; so that our joy consists wholly in the good pleasure of God, and His honor and glory are our sole contentment.

This foundation laid, the soul has but to pass her life rejoicing that God is God, abandoning herself so completely to His good pleasure that she is equally content to do one thing as another, according as this good pleasure directs, never even pausing to reflect upon the disposition which is made of her by the will of God.

Self-abandonment! this, then, is the grand duty which remains to be fulfilled after one has faithfully acquitted himself of all the obligations of his state. The perfection with which this grand duty is accomplished is the measure of one's sanctity.

A holy soul is a soul who, with the aid of grace, freely abandons herself to the divine will. All that follows this pure self-abandonment is the work of God and not of man. God asks nothing more of this soul than to blindly receive all that He sends, in a spirit of submission and universal indifference to the instruments of His will; the rest He determines and chooses according to His designs for the soul as an architect arranges and selects his materials according to the edifice he would construct.

In all things, therefore, we must love God and His order; we must love it as it is presented to us without desiring more. It is for God, not for us, to determine the objects of our submission, and what He sends is best for the soul. What a grand epitome of spirituality is this maxim of pure and absolute self-abandonment to the will of God! Self-abandonment, that continual forgetfulness of self which leaves the soul free to eternally love and obey God, untroubled by those fears, reflections, regrets, and anxieties which the care of one's own perfection and salvation gives! Since God offers to take upon Himself the care of our affairs, let us once for all abandon them to His infinite wisdom, that we may never more be occupied with aught but Him and His interests.

Arise, then, my soul; let us walk with uplifted head above all that is passing about us and within us, ever content with God—content with what He does with us, and with what He gives us to do. Let us beware of imprudently falling a prey to those numerous disquieting reflections which, like so many tangled labyrinths, entrap the mind into useless, endless wanderings. Let us avoid this snare of self-love by springing over it, and not by following its interminable windings.

Onward, my soul, through weariness, sickness, dryness, infirmities of temper, weakness of mind, snares of the devil and of men, their suspicions, jealousies, evil thoughts, and prejudices! Let us soar like the eagle above all these clouds, our eyes fixed upon the Sun of Justice, and its rays which are our obligations. Doubtless we may feel these trials; it does not depend upon us to be insensible to them. But let us remember that our life is not a life of sentiment. Let us live in this superior part of the soul where God and His will work out for us an ever uniform, equable, immutable eternity. In this wholly spiritual dwelling where the Uncreated, the Ineffable, the Infinite holds the soul immeasurably separated from all shadows and created atoms, reigns perpetual calm, even though the senses be the prey of tempests. We have learned to rise above the senses; their restlessness, their disquiet, their comings and goings, and their hundred transformations disturb us no more than the clouds which darken the sky for a moment and disappear. We know that in the region of the senses all things are like the wind, without sequence or order, in continual vicissitude. God's will forms the eternal charm of the heart in the state of faith, just as in the state of glory it shall constitute its true happiness; and this glorious state of the heart will influence the whole material being at present a prey to terrors and temptations. Under these appearances, however terrible they may be, the action of God, giving to the material being a facility wholly divine, will cause it to shine like the sun; for the faculties of the sensitive soul and those of the body are prepared here below like gold, iron, flax, and stone. And like these different substances they will attain the purity and splendor of their form only after they have passed through many processes and suffered loss and destruction. All that we endure here below at the hand of God is intended as a preparation for our future state.

The faithful soul who knows the secret of God's ways dwells in perfect peace; and all that transpires within her, so far from alarming, only reassures her. Intimately convinced that it is God who guides her, she accepts everything as a grace, and lives wholly forgetful of self, the object upon which God labors, that she may think only of the work committed to her care. Her love unceasingly animates the courage which enables her to faithfully and carefully fulfil her obligations.

Except the sins of a self-abandoned soul, which are light, and even converted to her good by the divine will, there is nothing *distinctly manifest* in her but the action of grace. And this action is distinctly manifest in all those painful or consoling impressions by means of which the divine will unceasingly works the soul's good. I use the term "distinctly manifest," for of all that transpires within the soul, these impressions are what it best distinguishes. To find God under all these appearances is the great art of faith; to make everything a means of uniting one's self with God is the exercise of faith.

CHAPTER II.

The more God seems to withdraw Light from the Soul abandoned to His Direction, the more Safely He guides Her.

It is particularly in souls wholly abandoned to God that the words of St. John are accomplished: *You have no need that any man teach you; but as His unction teacheth you of all things.* To know what God asks of them, they have but to consult this unction, to sound the heart, to heed its voice; it interprets the will of God according to their present needs. For the divine action disguised reveals its designs, not by thoughts, but by intuition. It manifests them to the soul either by necessity, leaving it but the one present course to choose, or by a first impulse, a sort of supernatural transport which impels to action without reflection, or, finally, by a certain attraction or repulsion which, while leaving the soul perfect liberty, no less attracts it to or withdraws it from objects.

Were we to judge by appearances, it would seem most unwise to thus pursue a course so uncertain; a course of conduct in which, according to ordinary rules, we find nothing stable, uniform, or regular. It is nevertheless at bottom the highest state of virtue, and one which usually is only attained after long exercise therein. The virtue of this state is virtue in all its purity; in fact, it is perfection. The soul is like a musician who to long practice unites great knowledge of music; he is so full of his art that, without any effort, all that he does therein is perfection; and if his compositions be examined, they will be found in perfect conformity with prescribed rules. One is convinced that he will never succeed better than when he acts without restraint, untrammelled by rules which fetter genius when too scrupulously followed; and his impromptus, like so many masterpieces, are the admiration of connoisseurs.

~ 75 ~

Thus the soul, after long exercise in the science and practice of perfection under the empire of reason and the methods with which she aids grace, insensibly forms a habit of acting in all things by divine instinct. Such a soul seems to intuitively accept as best the first duty that presents itself, without resorting to the reasoning which she formerly found necessary.

She has only to act according to circumstances, unable to do anything but abandon herself to that grace which can never mislead her. The work of a soul in this state of simplicity is nothing less than marvellous to eyes and minds divinely enlightened. Without rule, yet exactness itself; without measure, yet nothing better proportioned; without reflection, yet nothing more profound; without ingenuity, yet nothing better managed; without effort, yet nothing more efficacious; without forethought, yet nothing better fitted to unforeseen events.

The divine action frequently gives by means of spiritual reading knowledge which the authors never possessed. God makes use of the words and actions of others to inspire hidden truths. If He wills to enlighten us by such means, it is the part of the self-abandoned soul to accept them; and all means which become the instrument of the divine will possess an efficacy far surpassing their natural and apparent virtue.

A life of self-abandonment is characterized by mystery; it is a life which receives from God extraordinary miraculous gifts through commonplace, fortuitous events, chance encounters, where nothing is visible to human eyes but the ordinary workings of men's minds and the natural course of the elements. Thus the simplest sermons, the most commonplace conversations, the least elevating books, become to these souls by virtue of the will of God sources of intelligence and wisdom. Therefore they carefully gather the crumbs of wisdom which the worldly-wise trample under foot. Everything is precious to them, everything enriches them; so that, while supremely indifferent to all things, they neglect or despise nothing, drawing profit from all.

When we behold God in all things, and use them by His order, it is not using creatures, but enjoying the divine action which transmits its gifts through these different channels. They are not of themselves sanctifying, but only as instruments of the divine action which can and frequently does communicate its graces to simple souls by means apparently contrary to the end proposed. Yes, divine grace can enlighten with clay as with the most subtle material, and its instrument is always efficacious. All things are alike to it. Faith never feels any need; she complains not of the lack of means apparently necessary to her advancement, for the divine Workman for whom she labors supplies all deficiencies by His will. This holy will is the whole virtue of all creatures.

CHAPTER III.

The Afflictions with which God visits the Soul are but Loving Artifices at which she will One Day rejoice.

Souls who walk in light sing canticles of joy; those who walk amid shadows sing anthems of woe. Let one and the other sing to the end the portion and anthem God assigns them. We must add nothing to what He has completed. There must flow every drop of this gall of divine bitterness with which He wills to inebriate them. Behold Jeremias and Ezechiel: theirs was the language of sighs and lamentations, and their only consolation was in the continuation of their lament. He who would have dried their tears would have deprived us of the most beautiful portions of the Holy Scriptures. The spirit that afflicts is the only one which can console. The streams of sorrow and consolation flow from the same source.

When God astonishes a soul she must needs tremble; when He menaces, she cannot but fear. We have but to leave the divine operation to its own development; it bears within itself the remedy as well as the trial. Weep, dear souls; tremble, suffer disquiet and anguish; make no effort to escape these divine terrors, these heavenly lamentations. Receive into the depth of your being the waters of that sea of bitterness which inundated the soul of Christ. Continue to sow in tears at the will of divine grace, and insensibly by the same will their source shall be dried. The clouds will dissolve, the sun will shed its light, the springtime will strew your path with flowers, and your self-abandonment will manifest to you the whole extent of the admirable variety of the divine action.

Truly, man disquiets himself in vain! All that passes within him is like a dream. One shadow follows and effaces another, just as the fancies of sleep succeed one another, some troubling, others delighting, the mind. Man is the sport of these imaginations which consume one another, and the grand awakening will show the equal emptiness of them all. It will dissipate all illusions, and he will no longer heed the perils or fortunes of this dream called life.

Lord, can it not be said that Thy children sleep in Thy bosom during all the night of faith, while at Thy pleasure Thou fillest their souls with an infinite number and infinite variety of experiences which are in reality but holy and mysterious reveries? In this obscure night of the soul they are filled with veritable and awful terrors, with anguish and weariness which on the glorious day Thou wilt change into true and solid joys.

At their awakening, holy souls, restored to a clearer vision and fuller consciousness, will never weary admiring the skill, the art, the invention, the loving artifices of the Bridegroom. They will comprehend how impenetrable are His ways, how surpassing comprehension are His devices, how beyond discovery His disguises, how impossible consolation when He willed that they should mourn. On the day of this awakening the Jeremias and the Davids will see that that which wrought their bitterest pain was subject of rejoicing to God and the angels. Wake not the spouse, worldly-wise, industrious minds filled with self-activity; leave her to sigh and tremblingly seek for the Bridegroom. True, He eludes her, and disguises Himself; she sleeps, and her griefs are but as the phantoms which come with night and sleep. But disturb her not; let the Bridegroom work upon this cherished soul and depict in her what He alone can paint or express. Leave Him to develop the result of this state. He will awake her when it is time. Joseph causes Benjamin to weep; servants of Joseph, reveal not his secret to this cherished brother! The artifice of Joseph is beyond the penetration of Benjamin. He and his poor brothers are plunged in grief; they see naught in the loving artifice of Joseph but irremediable suffering. Enlighten them not: He will remedy all; He will reveal himself to them, and they will admire the wisdom of Him who out of so much woe and desolation wrought the truest joy they have ever known.

CHAPTER IV.

The more God seems to take from a Soul wholly abandoned to Him, the more Generous He is to her.

But let us go on in the study of the divine action and its loving artifices. What the divine action seems to take from a good will it gives in *disguise*, so to speak. It never leaves a good will in need. For example, if we relieved the necessities of a friend with generous gifts, allowing him to know they came from us, but later, in his interest making a feint of withholding our gifts while continuing to secretly assist him, the friend, not suspecting the ruse or comprehending the kindly artifice, is grieved and hurt. Bitter reflections and unkind thoughts of his benefactor torment him. But when the loving ruse is revealed to him, imagine the joy, the confusion, the love, the shame, the gratitude, which overwhelm him! And are not his zeal and love for his benefactor greater henceforth? And has not the trial only strengthened his love and made it proof against any similar misunderstandings in the future?

The application is simple. The more we seem to lose with God, the more we really gain; the more He deprives us of natural aid, the more He gives us of supernatural. We loved Him a little for His gifts, but these being no longer visible we come to love Him for Himself. It is by the apparent withdrawal of these sensible gifts and favors that He prepares us for Himself, the greatest of all gifts. The souls once wholly submissive to the divine action should always interpret all things favorably—yes, were it the loss of the most excellent of directors, were it the distrust which they feel in spite of themselves for those who too readily offer to fill his place; for usually the guides who of themselves seek the direction of souls merit a little distrust. Those who are truly animated by the Spirit of God are not ordinarily so impetuous or self-confident: they are sought, they do not offer themselves, and never cease to distrust themselves.

Let the soul that has wholly given herself to God walk fearlessly through all these trials, letting none of them deprive her of her liberty. Provided she be faithful to the divine action, this all-powerful action will work wonders in her despite all obstacles. God and the soul are engaged in the same work, the success of which, though depending entirely on the action of the divine Workman, may nevertheless be compromised by the infidelity of the soul.

When it is well with the soul, all goes well; for that which is of God—that is, His part and action—are, so to speak, the rebound of the soul's fidelity. It is the right side of the work which, like those famous tapestries, are done stitch by stitch on the wrong side. The workman engaged thereon sees but his needle and the canvas, every little hole of which is successively filled, forming a beautiful design which is only visible however, when every detail is completed, and the right side is held up to view, but during the process of the work all its beauty and its marvels were unseen.

And thus it is with the self-abandoned soul: it sees only God and its duty. The fulfilment of the duty of each moment is but the addition of an imperceptible point, and yet it is by means of these apparent trifles that God effects His wonders. We are given a presentment of these wonders at times here below, but we shall only understand them in the light of eternity. How full of wisdom and goodness are the ways of God! He has made all that is great, elevating and ennobling so completely the work of His grace and action, leaving to the soul what is easy and simple to be accomplished with the aid of grace, that there is no one who cannot attain eminent sanctity by the loving fulfilment of obscure and humble duties.

CHAPTER V.

The less Capable the Faithful Soul is of defending Herself, the more Powerfully does God defend Her.

The supreme and infallible work of the divine action is always opportunely applied to the simple soul, and she in all things wisely corresponds to its intimate direction. She accepts all that comes to her, all that transpires, all that she feels—all, all save sin; sometimes consciously, sometimes unconsciously, being impelled, not by any reason, but by an indistinct impulse, to speak, to act, or not to act.

Frequently the occasion and the reason which determine her course are merely of the natural order; the simple soul sees no mystery therein, but pure chance, necessity, conventionality; it is nothing in her eyes or those of others: and yet the divine action, which is the wisdom, the counsel, the knowledge of its friends, causes these simple things to work their good. It appropriates them and turns them so energetically against the schemes of the faithful soul's enemies, that it is impossible for them to injure her.

The divine action frees the soul from the petty anxious schemes so necessary to human prudence. Such precautions are suitable for Herod and the Pharisees: but the Magi have but to follow their star in peace; the Babe has but to rest in His Mother's arms; His enemies advance His cause more than they injure it; the more they seek to thwart and overwhelm it, the more peacefully and freely He advances. He will not court or temporize with them to turn their attacks from Him; their jealousies, their distrust, their persecutions, are necessary to Him. Thus lived Jesus in Judea; and He still lives after this manner in simple souls, where He is generous, gentle, free, peaceful; fearing and needing no creature, but beholding them all in the hands of His Father; eager to turn them to His service, some through their criminal passions, others through their good actions, others through their obedience and submission.

The divine action marvellously adjusts all these things: there is neither too little nor too much; no more good and evil than needful.

The order of God sends each moment the appropriate instrument for its work; and the simple soul enlightened by faith finds all things good, desiring neither more nor less than she possesses. At all times she blesses the divine Hand which so carefully supplies her needs and frees her from obstacles; she receives friends and foes with equal sweetness, for it is the way of Jesus to treat the whole world as a divine instrument. We want for none, and yet we have need of all; the divine action renders all necessary, and we must receive all from it, accepting each thing according to its nature and quality, and corresponding thereto with sweetness and humility, treating the simple with simplicity, the ungentle with gentleness, after the teaching of St. Paul and the more beautiful practice of the divine Master.

Divine grace alone can imprint that supernatural character which adapts itself so marvellously to each individual nature. It is not learned from books; it is a true spirit of prophecy, and the effect of intimate revelation; it is the teaching of the Holy Spirit. To conceive it one must have attained the highest degree of self-abandonment and the most perfect detachment from all plans and interests, however holy they may be. We must keep before our eyes the one important thing in this world, viz., the passive abandonment to the divine action which is required of us in order to devote ourselves to the duties of our state, leaving the Holy Spirit to operate interiorly, indifferent as to what He operates upon, even happy not to know it. Then, then we are safe; for all the events of the world can only work the good of souls perfectly submissive to the divine will of God.

CHAPTER VI.

The Soul abandoned to the Will of God, so far from resisting her Enemies, finds in them Useful Auxiliaries.

I fear my own action and that of my friends more than I do my enemies. There is no prudence equal to that of offering no resistance to one's enemies but that of simple abandonment to the will of God; nothing which so fully insures our peace; it is rowing with the tide, sailing with a wind which swiftly brings us into port. There is nothing better than simplicity with which to meet the prudence of this world; it skilfully, though unconsciously, evades its snares without even thinking of them.

Dealing with a simple soul is, in a measure, dealing with God. Who can cope with the Almighty, whose ways are inscrutable? God espouses the cause of the simple soul; she has no need to study the intrigues of her enemies, to meet their activity with equal alertness, watching all their movements: her Spouse relieves her of all this; she confides all to Him, and then rests on His breast in peace and security. The divine action inspires her with measures so just that they who sought to surprise her are themselves surprised. She benefits by all their efforts, and rises by the very means with which they sought to abase her. All contradictions turn to her good; and by leaving her enemies to work their will she draws so great and continual profit from them that all she need fear is that she may interfere in a work in which God wills to be the chief actor, using her enemies as His instruments, and in which the soul has no other part than to peacefully watch the working of the divine will and follow its guidance with simplicity.

The supernatural prudence of the divine Spirit, the principle of these attractions, unerringly seizes the end and intimate relations of each event, and, all unknown to the soul, so disposes them for her spiritual welfare that all which opposes itself thereto must inevitably be destroyed.

CHAPTER VII.

The Soul who abandons Herself to God has no Need to justify Herself by Words or Actions: the Divine Action justifies Her.

The broad, solid, firm rock upon which the faithful soul stands sheltered from tides and storms is the order of the divine will, which is ever present with us, veiled under crosses or the most ordinary duties. Behind these shadows is hidden God's Hand, which sustains and upholds those who abandon themselves to Him.

The moment the soul is firmly established in this perfect self-abandonment she is henceforth safe from the contradiction of tongues, for she ceases to have anything to do or say in her own defence. Since the work is God's, from no other source must its justification be sought. Its consequences and effects will sufficiently justify it. We have but to leave it to its own development. *Dies diei eructat verbum.*

When we are no longer guided by our own ideas we need not defend ourselves by words. Our words can only represent our ideas, and where an absence of ideas is admitted no words are needed. Of what avail are they? To give a reason for what we do? But we know not this reason; it is hidden in the principle which animates our actions, and which impresses us only in a most ineffable manner.

We must therefore leave to the results of our actions the task of justifying their principle. All is metely sustained in this divine procession; everything therein has a firm and solid basis, and the reason for that which precedes is manifest in the result which follows. It is no longer a life of thought, imagination, multiplied words: these no longer occupy, nourish, or sustain the soul. She no longer knows where she walks, or where her path may lie in the future; she ceases to incite herself with reflections to bear the toils and fatigues of the route; her strength lies in an intimate conviction of her own weakness. A way is opened to her feet; she enters and walks unhesitatingly therein with pure, straightforward, simple faith; she follows the straight path of the commandments, leaning upon God Himself, whom she finds at every turn of the way; and this God, the sole object of her life, will take her justification upon Himself, and so manifest His presence that she will be avenged of her detractors.

CHAPTER VIII.

God gives Life to the Soul abandoned to Him by Means which apparently lead only to Death.

There is a time when God wills to be the life of the soul and work out her perfection Himself in a hidden and secret manner: then all her own ideas, lights, efforts, researches, reasonings, become a source of illusion. And when the soul, after many sad experiences, is finally taught the uselessness of her self-activity, she finds that God has hidden and obstructed all other channels of life that she may live in Him alone. Then, convinced of her nothingness, and that her self-activity is prejudicial to her, she abandons herself completely to God and relies only upon Him. God then becomes a source of life to the soul, not by means of thoughts, revelations, reflections (these are now become a source of illusion), but effectively by the reality of His grace hidden under the strangest appearances. The divine operation being invisible to the soul, she receives its virtue, its substance, under circumstances which she feels will prove her ruin. There is no remedy for this obscurity; we must remain buried therein; for here, in this night of faith, God gives Himself to us, and with Himself all things. Henceforth the soul is but a blind subject; or rather she may be likened to a sick man who, ignorant of the virtue of his remedies, and feeling only their bitterness, frequently imagines they must lead to death; the exhaustion and crisis which follow them seem to justify his fears: nevertheless, under this semblance of death he receives health, and he continues to accept the remedies at the word of the physician.

Thus souls abandoned to God's will take no heed of their infirmities, except those of a nature sufficiently evident and grave to require care and treatment. The languor and impotence of faithful souls are but illusions and semblances which they must courageously face. God sends and permits them to exercise their faith and self-abandonment, and in these virtues lies the soul's true remedy. She must go on generously, utterly ignoring her infirmities, accepting all that comes to her to do or suffer in the order of God, never hesitating to treat her body as we do those beasts of burden only destined to spend their lives going hither and thither at our will. This treatment is more efficacious than all that delicate care which only weakens the vigor of the mind. This strength of purpose has an indescribable virtue and power to sustain a feeble body; and a year of this noble and generous life is worth a century of selfish fears and care.

We must endeavor to habitually maintain an air of childlike gentleness and good-will. Ah! what can we fear from this divine fortune? Guided, sustained, and protected by the Providence of God, the whole exterior conduct of His children should be nothing less than heroic. The alarming objects which oppose their progress are naught in themselves: they are only sent to embellish their lives by still more glorious actions. They entangle them in embarrassments of every kind, whence human prudence can see no issue, and, feeling its weakness, stops short, confounded. Then does the divine fortune gloriously manifest what it is for souls who wholly trust therein. It extricates them more marvellously than the writers of fiction with unrestrained imagination in the leisure and privacy of their study unraveled the intrigues and perils of their imaginary heroes, bringing them invariably to a happy end. More admirably still does it guide them safely through the perils of death, the snares of demons, the terrors of temptation, the fears of hell. It elevates these souls to heaven, and they are all the real subject of those mystic histories more beautiful and curious than any ever invented by the crude imagination of man.

Then onward, my soul, through perils and fears, guided, directed, and sustained by the invisible, all-powerful, unerring Hand of divine Providence. Let us go on fearlessly in joy and peace to the end, turning obstacles into victories, remembering that it was to struggle and conquer that we enrolled ourselves under His banner. *Exivit vincens ut vinceret*, and every step under His guidance is a victory. The book of souls lies open before the Holy Spirit, and their history is still written, for holy souls will furnish material for its pages to the end of the world. This history is but the relation of God's operations and designs upon man, and it depends upon ourselves whether we shall appear in its pages and continue its narration by uniting our sufferings and actions to His divine will.

No; let nothing we have to do or suffer alarm us: it can cause us no loss; it is only sent us that we may furnish material for that holy history, which is increasing day by day.

CHAPTER IX.

Love holds the Place of All Things to Souls who walk in the Way of Abandonment.

God, while He despoils a soul who wholly abandons herself to Him, gives her something which takes the place of all things—of light, of strength, of life, of wisdom. This gift is His love. Divine love is like a supernatural instinct in these souls.

Everything in nature has that which is suited to its kind; each flower has its peculiar charm, each animal its instinct, and each creature its perfection. And so it is in the different states of grace; each has its special grace, and this is a recompense to every one whose good will brings him in harmony with the state in which Providence has placed him.

A soul becomes subject to the divine action the moment a good will is formed in her heart; and this action influences her according to the degree of her self-abandonment. The art of self-abandonment is simply the art of loving; divine love grants all things to the soul who refuses Him nothing. And as God's love inspires the desires of a soul who lives for him, He can never refuse them; therefore, cannot love desire what it pleases?

The divine action only considers the good will of a soul; the capacity or incapacity of the other faculties neither attract nor repel it. If it find a soul good, pure, upright, simple, submissive, it is all it requires; it takes possession of this soul and of all her faculties, and so disposes all things for her good that she finds means of sanctification in everything. That which would give death to others, should it enter this soul will be harmless, for the antidote of her good will will arrest the effect of the poison. If she stray to the brink of the abyss, the divine action will withhold her from its depths, or if she fall it will rescue her. And indeed the faults of these souls are but faults of frailty and little perceptible; God's love knows how to turn them to her advantage, and by secret and ineffable ways teaches her what she should say and do according to the circumstances in which she is placed.

Such souls receive as it were rays of divine intelligence: *Intellectus bonus omnibus facientibus eum.* For this divine intelligence accompanies them in all their wanderings, and rescues them from the snares into which their simplicity leads them. Have they committed themselves by some mistaken measure? Providence disposes a happy event which releases them. Vainly are intrigues multiplied against them; Providence overcomes all the efforts of their enemies, and so confounds and bewilders them that they fall into their own snares. Do they seek to surprise the soul? Providence, by means of some apparently unimportant action which she unconsciously performs, rescues her from the embarrassments into which she has been led by her own uprightness and the malice of her enemies.

Oh, the exquisite wisdom of this good will! What prudence in its simplicity, what ingenuity in its innocence, what frankness in its mysteries, what mystery in its candor!

Behold the young Tobias: he is a mere youth; but Raphael walks at his side, and with such a guide he walks in safety, he feels no want, nothing affrights him. Even the monsters he encounters furnish him food and healing; the very creature which springs to devour him becomes his nourishment. He is only occupied with nuptials and festivities, for such is his present duty in the order of Providence; not that he is without other cares, but they are abandoned to that divine intelligence charged to assist him in all things; and the result of his affairs is better than he could have made it, for everything succeeds and is crowned with prosperity. Yet the mother bitterly grieves, while the father is full of faith; but the child so sorely lamented joyfully returns to become the happiness of his family.

Then for those souls who wholly abandon themselves to it, divine love is the source of all good; and an earnest desire is all that is necessary to obtain this inestimable blessing.

Yes, dear souls, God asks but your heart; if you seek you will find this treasure, this kingdom where God alone reigns.

If your heart be wholly devoted to God, within it you will find the treasure, the kingdom itself, which is the object of your desires. The moment we desire God and His will, that moment we enjoy them, and our enjoyment corresponds to the ardor of our desires. The earnest desire to love God is loving Him. Because we love Him we desire to be the instruments of His action, that His love may freely operate in us and through us.

The work of the divine action is not in proportion to the capacity of a simple holy soul, but to her purity of intention; nor does it correspond to the means she adopts, the projects she forms, the counsel she follows. The soul may err in all these, and this not rarely happens; but with a good will and pure intention she can never be misled. When God sees this good disposition He overlooks all the rest, and accepts as done what the soul would assuredly do if circumstances seconded her good will.

Therefore a good will has nothing to fear; if it falter, it can but fall under that all-powerful Hand which guides and sustains it in all its wanderings. It is this divine Hand which draws it towards the goal when it has wandered therefrom, which restores it to the path whence its feet have strayed; it is the soul's refuge in the difficulties into which the efforts of her blind faculties lead her; and the soul learns to despise these, efforts to wholly abandon herself to the infallible guidance of this divine Hand. Even the errors of these good souls lead them to self-abandonment; and never will a good will find itself unaided, for it is a dogma of faith that *all things work the good* of such souls.

CHAPTER X.

The Faithful Soul finds in Submission to the Will of God more Force and Strength than the Proudest of those who resist Him.

What avail the most sublime intelligence and divine revelations if we love not the will of God? It was through these that Lucifer perished. The work of the divine action which God revealed to him in the mystery of the Incarnation excited only his envy. A simple soul, on the contrary, enlightened by faith alone, never wearies admiring, praising, and loving the order of God, recognizing it not only in holy things, but even amid the greatest confusion and disorder of events. A simple soul is more enlightened with a ray of pure faith than was Lucifer by His sublime revelations.

The science of a soul faithful to her obligations, peacefully submissive to the secret inspirations of grace, humble and gentle with all, is worth more than the profound wisdom which penetrates mysteries.

If we would learn to see but the will of God in the pride and cruelty of creatures, we would always meet them with gentleness and respect. Whatever the consequences of their disorders, they can never mar the divine order. We must only see in creatures the will of God, whose instruments they are, and whose grace they communicate to us when we receive them with meekness and humility. We have not to concern ourselves for their course, but keep steadily on in our own; and thus, with gentle firmness, we will triumph over all obstacles, were they firmly rooted as cedars and irresistible as rocks.

What can resist the force of a meek, humble, faithful soul? If we would vanquish all our adversaries, we have but to use the weapons God has placed in our hands. He has given them for our defence, and there is nothing to be feared in using them. We must not be cowardly but generous, as becomes souls chosen to do God's work. God's workings are sublime and marvellous; and never can human action, warring upon God, resist one who is united to the divine will by the practice of meekness and humility.

What was Lucifer? A beautiful spirit, more enlightened than all the others; but a beautiful spirit rebellious against God and His will.

The mystery of evil is but the continuation of this rebellion in every variety of form. Lucifer, as far as lies in his power, would subvert all that God has done and ordained. Wherever he penetrates, God's work is marred. The greater one's learning, science, understanding, the greater his danger if he possess not that foundation of piety which consists in submission to the will of God. It is a disciplined, submissive heart which unites us to the divine action; without it all our goodness is but natural virtue, and ordinarily in opposition to the order of God. This all-powerful Workman only recognizes the humble as His instruments, and condemns the rebellious proud to serve in spite of themselves as the slaves of divine justice.

When I see a soul whose first object is God and submission to His will, however much she may be lacking in other things, I say, Here is a soul with great talents for serving God. The Blessed Virgin and St. Joseph appear to have been after this model. Other gifts without this alarm me; I fear to see the action of Lucifer repeated. I am on my guard, and intrench myself in my simplicity to resist the dazzling splendor of those gifts, of themselves so perishable and fragile.

CHAPTER XI.

The Soul abandoned to God learns to recognize His Will even in the Proud who resist Him. All Creatures, whether Good or Evil, reveal Him to her.

The will of God is the whole life of the simple soul. She respects this will even in the evil actions by which the proud seek to abase her. The proud despise a soul in whose eyes they are nothing; for she sees only God in them and all their actions. Frequently they mistake her humble demeanor for awe of themselves, when it is only a mark of her loving fear of God and His will which is present to her in the proud.

No, poor foolish creatures, the simple soul fears ye not. Rather, she compassionates you. It is to God she speaks when she seems to address you; it is with Him she treats; she regards you only as His slaves, or rather as shadows which veil Him. Therefore, the more overbearing you are, the more humble she becomes; and when you think to entrap her you find yourselves the dupes. Your diplomacy, your violence, are to her, but favors of Providence. Yes, the proud are still an enigma which the simple soul enlightened by faith clearly reads.

This recognition of the divine will in all that transpires each moment within us and about us is the true science of the spiritual life; it is a continual revelation of truth; it is a communication with God incessantly renewed; it is the enjoyment of the Bridegroom, not covertly, secretly, in the "clefts of the rock," in the "vineyard," but openly, publicly, without fear of creatures. It is a depth of peace, joy, love, and contentment with God, whom we see, or rather behold, through faith, living and working the perfection of each event. It is the eternal paradise, now tasted, it is true, only in things incomplete and veiled in obscurity; but the Spirit of God disposes all the events of this life by the fruitful omnipresence of His action, and on the last day He will say, *Let there be light* (*Fiat lux*); and then shall be revealed the treasures of that abyss of peace and contentment with God which each action, each cross, conceals.

When God thus gives Himself to a soul, all that is ordinary becomes extraordinary; therefore it is that nothing appears of the great work which is going on in the soul; the way itself is so marvellous that it needs not the embellishment of marvels which belong not to it. It is a miracle, a revelation, a continuous enjoyment of God, interrupted only by little faults; but in itself it is characterized by the absence of anything sensible or marvellous, while it renders marvellous all ordinary and sensible things.

CHAPTER XII.

God assures to Faithful Souls a Glorious Victory over the Powers of Earth and Hell.

If the divine action is veiled here below by an exterior of weakness, it is that the merit of faithful souls may be increased; but its triumph is no less sure. The history of the world is simply the history of the struggle maintained from the beginning by the powers of the world and hell with souls humbly submissive to the divine action. In the conflict all the advantage seems to be on the side of the proud; yet humility is always victorious.

This world is represented to us under the form of a statue of gold, brass, iron, and clay. This mystery of iniquity which was shown in a dream to Nebuchadnezzar is but the confused assemblage of all the acts, interior and exterior, of the children of darkness. These are again represented by the beast coming up out of the abyss from the beginning of all ages, to make war upon the interior and spiritual man; and this war still continues. The monsters succeed one another; the abyss swallows them and vomits them forth again, while unceasingly emitting new and strange vapors. The combat begun in heaven between Lucifer and St. Michael still wages. The heart of that proud and envious spirit has become an inexhaustible abyss of every kind of evil; and his only aim since the creation of the world has been to ever raise up among men new workers of iniquity to replace those swallowed up in the abyss. Lucifer is the chieftain of those who refuse obedience to the Almighty; this mystery of iniquity is but the inversion of the order of God. It is the order, or rather the disorder, of Satan. This disorder is a mystery, for beneath a fair exterior it hides irremediable infinite evils. All the wicked who have declared war against God, from Cain to those who now lay waste the earth, have been seemingly great and powerful princes, famous in the world and worshipped of men. But their apparent splendor is a portion of the mystery; they are but the beasts which, one after another, rise from the abyss to subvert the order of God. But this order, which is another mystery, resists them with men truly powerful and great, who give the death-blow to these monsters; and even as hell vomits forth new monsters, heaven raises up new heroes to battle with them. Ancient history, sacred and profane, is but the record of this war. The will of God always triumphs. His followers share His victories and reap a happy eternity. But iniquity can never protect its followers, and the deserters from God's cause reap death, eternal death.

The wicked ever believe themselves invincible; but oh, my God, who shall resist Thee! Were the powers of earth and hell ranged against one single soul, she would have naught to fear in abandoning herself to the will of God. That apparent might and irresistible power of iniquity, that head of gold, that body of silver, brass, and iron, is but a phantom of glittering dust. A pebble overthrows it and makes it the sport of the winds.

How admirable is the work of the Holy Spirit throughout all ages! The revolutions which irresistibly carry men along with them, the brilliant heroes heralded with so much pomp, who shine like stars above the rest of mankind, the marvels of the age, are all but as the dream of Nebuchadnezzar, which at his awakening fled with all its terrors.

All these things are only sent to exercise the courage of the children of God; and when their virtue is proved and confirmed, He permits them to overcome these monsters, and continues to send new warriors into the field. So that this life is a continual warfare which exercises the courage of the saints on earth, and causes joy in heaven and confusion in hell.

Thus all opposition to the will, the order of God, serves but to render it more adorable. The servers of iniquity are the slaves of justice, and from the ruins of Babylon the divine action builds the heavenly Jerusalem.

APPENDIX.

Our readers will be grateful to us for adding to Father Caussade's treatise a few methods which facilitate the practice of abandonment. To recommend these methods it suffices to say that their authors are St. Francis de Sales, Saint Jane Frances de Chantal, Bossuet, and Father Surin.

I. A very easy Means of acquiring Peace of Heart.

By Father Surin, S. J.

It seems to me that the multiplicity of methods we employ to acquire and practise virtue is one of the obstacles to our being solidly established therein. Not that I counsel being so irrevocably bound to one method that we are not ready to change when God's attraction changes. But, after all, this attraction at bottom never changes, and only presents itself under a more spiritual form. They who will be faithful to the following rules will have no difficulty in practising the virtues appropriate to the circumstances, the time, and the place in which they find themselves, and in relishing in the exercise of these virtues the peace and holy liberty of the children of God.

1st. Let us be fully convinced that we have but one thing to do: to possess each moment the fulness of our mind, without permitting the reasonable will to uselessly recall the past or excite vain anxieties concerning the future.

True abandonment, which makes God look upon us with love, consists in leaving the past to His ever merciful justice, and in confiding the future to His fatherly Providence. The remembrance of our past infidelities should humble but not trouble us, though we were convinced that they are much more serious than they appear.

In regard to the future, let us place no trust whatever in our strength and the sentiments of devotion we may experience; let us place all our trust in Jesus alone, however contrary sensible impressions may be. Relying on this foundation, it is no presumption to feel ourselves stronger than earth and hell; and the greater this confidence, the more it honors Jesus Christ, and the more it disposes His goodness to succor us in all our needs.

2d. We shall sanctify the present moment by renewing as frequently as we shall feel it needful the act of recollection which we must have made the first time with all the fervor of which we are capable; but this recollection should be very peaceful and dwell in the depths of the soul more than in the sensible part.

3d. We can remain faithful to this recollection only on condition that we frequently examine the interior and exterior condition of our soul. As soon as we discover in her any irregularity, however small, or in any degree displeasing to God, we should proceed to restore order with a heart as tranquil as if we had never failed, without disquieting ourselves with reflections springing from self-love, vexation at the fault committed, or from a pretext of livelier contrition. These sentiments can only retard our progress in virtue; for, while the soul amuses itself caressing its chagrin and probing its past faults, this useless introspection paralyzes its action and disposes it to new falls. A peaceful regret for time ill employed, united with an earnest endeavor to make better use of the present moment, is the true character of love of God.

4th. The quickest means of attaining peace of heart is love of our own abjection and miseries, voluntary offence against God, however, excepted. This love of one's personal abjection derives profit from everything, even from falls, which should never discourage us.

A soul that loves her own abjection laughs at discouragement and combats it with all her strength. Content to be of herself but impotence and misery, she rejoices that Jesus Christ possesses the fulness of all perfection, and that she cannot do without Him an instant. She would not, were it in her power, will to have any strength of herself, for her radical impotence for all good and her unceasing need of Jesus Christ set forth His divine attributes to greater advantage. This is the sole contentment of a soul that seeks only the glory of God.

In this peaceful, humble way we advance in purity of divine love, and in the extermination of our bad habits more rapidly in a week than we would in a year of unquiet vigilance. Very little experience of God's way will convince us of this. For self-love is the motive and end of those who yield to disquiet, while those who proceed with the calmness of which we have spoken rely on Jesus Christ. Now, it is most evident that seeking only God's interest always gives strength, and that egotism, even spiritual egotism, being a disorder, is weakening.

5th. The perfection of order is to be found in the complete fusion of our interests with those of God. Therefore he who remains faithful to this sweet habit is not astonished to see himself assailed by every form of temptation; he bears the weary burden of them as the natural fruit of his misery, maintains in the depth of his heart a resigned acquiescence, and courageously drags this weary chain of his past without permitting himself to be troubled or cast down by the memory of his iniquities. When this thought assails him, he loses no time examining whence it came, nor how long it has lasted, for such an examination would be in itself a new distraction, more voluntary and injurious than the first; he is satisfied with humbling himself at sight of this infidelity, which, wholly involuntary as it is, proves, nevertheless, that his heart is not wholly fixed upon God. Disquietude in this case being a mark of self-love, we must return to God and seek peace in love of our own abjection.

6th. We must follow the same rule in our relations with our neighbor, and cause him to feel the truth of these words of our Saviour: "My yoke is sweet, and My burden light." No one who takes this yoke upon himself can fail to realize these words, for they are the utterance of eternal Truth. The practice of which we have just spoken will inevitably cause us to taste its sweetness.

7th. When this feeling of disquiet has passed, and peace of mind is restored, it is well then to recall our past faults in order to humble and reprove ourselves. There is no one who should not feel the need of doing this, so great is the depth of our pride and self-love which never die, and never cease alas! to produce new fruits. If we neglect this very important point, the foundation of our virtues will inevitably lose its solidity. When, on the contrary, we persevere in this habit, we always conceive a greater esteem for our neighbor; unfavorable appearances no longer lead us to judge rashly, and we only condemn ourselves, for, recognizing our nothingness and sinfulness, we place ourselves under the feet of all.

8th. In considering our past faults, we must first see how we could have avoided falling; then with a tranquil heart lay before Jesus our misery and the will to be faithful to Him which He gives us; finally, we must not vainly amuse ourselves with estimating the difficulty or the facility we experience in doing good. We must not go to God circuitously, but unceasingly rouse ourselves to that pure and generous disinterestedness which will lead us directly to His most loving and adorable Majesty.

II. On Perfect Abandonment.

By Bossuet.

When we are truly abandoned to God's will, we are ready for all that may come to us: we suppose the worst that can be supposed, and we cast ourselves blindly on the bosom of God. We forget ourselves, we lose ourselves: and this entire forgetfulness of self is the most perfect penance we can perform; for all conversion consists only in truly renouncing and forgetting ourselves, to be occupied with God and filled with Him. This forgetfulness of self is the martyrdom of self-love; it is its death, and an annihilation which leaves it without resources: then the heart dilates and is enlarged. We are relieved by casting from us the dangerous weight of self which formerly overwhelmed us. We look upon God as a good Father who leads us, as it were, by the hand in the present moment; and all our rest is in humble and firm confidence in His fatherly goodness.

If anything is capable of making a heart free and unrestrained, it is perfect abandonment to God and His holy will: this abandonment fills the heart with a divine peace more abundant than the fullest and vastest floods. If anything can render a mind serene, dissipate the keenest anxieties, soften the bitterest pains, it is assuredly this perfect simplicity and liberty of a heart wholly abandoned to the hands of God. The unction of abandonment gives a certain vigor to all the actions, and spreads the joy of the Holy Spirit even over the countenance and words. I will place all my strength, therefore, in this perfect abandonment to God's hands, through Jesus Christ, and He will be my conclusion in all things in virtue of the Holy Spirit. Amen.

III. A Short and Easy Method of making the Prayer of Faith, and of the Simple Presence of God.

By Bossuet.

1st. We must accustom ourselves to nourish our soul with a simple and loving thought of God, and of Jesus Christ, our Lord; and to this end we must gently separate her from all discourse, reasoning, and a multitude of affections, to keep her in simplicity, respect, and attention, and thus bring her nearer and nearer to God, her sole and sovereign good, her first principle, and her last end.

2d. The perfection of this life consists in union with our Sovereign Good; and the greater the simplicity, the more perfect the union. It is for this reason that those who would be perfect are interiorly solicited by grace to become simple, that they may finally be capable of enjoying the *one thing* necessary—that is, eternal unity. Then let us frequently say, in the depth of our hearts: *O unum necessarium, unum volo, unum quæro, unum mihi est necessarium, Deus meus et omnia.* (Oh, one thing necessary! Thee alone do I wish, do I seek, do I desire! Thou art all that I need, O my God and my all!)

3d. Meditation is very good in its time, and very useful at the beginning of the spiritual life; but we must not stop at it, as the soul by her fidelity to mortification, and recollection, usually receives a purer and more intimate form of prayer which may be called the prayer of "simplicity." It consists in a simple and loving attention, or contemplation of some divine object, either of God in Himself or some of His perfections, or of Jesus Christ or some of His mysteries, or some other of the Christian truths. Then the soul, abandoning all reasoning, falls into a sweet contemplation which keeps her tranquil, attentive, and susceptible of the operations and the divine impressions which the Holy Spirit communicates to her: she does little, and receives much; her labor is sweet, and yet most fruitful; and as she approaches nearer to the source of all light, all grace, all virtue, she also receives more.

4th. The practice of this prayer should begin at our awakening by an act of faith in the presence of God, who is everywhere, and in Jesus Christ, whose eyes never leave us though we were buried in the centre of the earth. This act is made sensibly, in the usual manner; for example, by saying interiorly, "I believe that my God is present;" or by a simple thought of faith in God present with us, which is a purer and more spiritual act.

5th. Then we must not endeavor to multiply, or produce several other acts or various dispositions, but remain simply attentive to this presence of God, exposed to this divine radiance, thus continuing this devout attention or exposition as long as God gives us the grace of it, without being eager to make other acts than those with which we are inspired, since this prayer is a prayer with God alone, and a union which eminently contains all the other special dispositions; and which disposes the soul to passiveness; that is to say, God becomes sole master of her interior, and there effects more special work. The less the creature labors in this state, the more powerfully God acts in her; and since the operation of God is a repose, the soul, in this prayer, becomes in a manner like Him, and receives, also, marvellous effects; and as the rays of the sun cause the plants to grow and blossom and bear fruit, so the attentive soul, exposed in tranquillity to the rays of the divine Sun of justice, more effectually imbibes the divine influences which enrich her with all virtues.

6th. The continuation of this attention in faith will serve her as thanksgiving for all the graces received during the night, and throughout her life, as an offering of herself and all her actions, as a direction of her intention, etc.

7th. The soul may fear to lose much by the omission of other acts, but experience will teach her, on the contrary, that she gains a great deal; for the greater her knowledge of God, the greater also will be the purity of her love, of her intentions, the greater will be her detestation of sin, and the greater and more continual her recollection, mortification, and humility.

8th. This will not prevent her from making other interior or exterior acts of virtue when she feels herself impelled thereto by grace; but the fundamental and usual state of her interior should be that union with God which will keep her abandoned to His hands and delivered up to His love, to quietly accomplish all His will.

9th. The time of meditation being come, we must begin it with great respect by a simple recollection of God, invoking His Spirit, and uniting ourselves intimately with Jesus Christ; then continue it in this same way. It will be the same with vocal prayers, office, and the Holy Sacrifice, whether we celebrate it or assist at it. Even the examination of conscience should be made after no other method: this same light which keeps our attention upon God will cause us to discover our slightest imperfections, and deeply deplore and regret them. We should go to table with the same spirit of simplicity which will keep us more occupied with God than with the repast, and leave us free to give better attention to what is being read. This practice binds us to nothing but to keep our soul detached from all imperfection, and attached only to God and intimately united with Him, in which consists all our welfare.

10th. We should take our recreation in the same disposition, to give the body and mind relaxation without permitting ourselves the dissipation of curious news, immoderate laughter, nor any indiscreet word, etc.; always keeping ourselves pure and free interiorly without disturbing others, frequently uniting ourselves to God by a simple and loving thought of Him; remembering that we are in His presence, and that He does not wish us to be separated at any moment from Him and His holy will. The most ordinary rule of this state of simplicity and the sovereign disposition of the soul is to do the will of God in all things. Regarding all as coming from God and going from all to God, is what sustains and fortifies the soul in all its occupations and in all that comes to it, and maintains us in the possession of simplicity. Then let us always follow the will of God, after the example of Jesus Christ, and united to Him as our Head. This is an excellent means of making progress in this manner of prayer, in order to attain through it to the most solid virtue and the most perfect sanctity.

11th. We should console ourselves in the same manner, and preserve this simple and intimate union with God in all our actions—in the parlor, in the cell, at table, at recreation. Let us add, that in all our intercourse we should endeavor to edify our neighbor, by taking advantage of every occasion to lead one another to piety, the love of God, the practice of good works, in order that we may diffuse the good odor of Jesus Christ. *If any man speak*, says St. Peter, *let him speak as the words of God,* and as if God Himself spoke through him. To do this, it suffices to follow the inspiration of the Holy Spirit: He will inspire you as to that which is simply and unaffectedly suitable at all times.

Finally, we will finish the day by animating with the sentiment of this holy presence our examen, evening prayer, and preparations for rest; and we will go to sleep with this loving attention, interspersing our rest, when we awake during the night, with a few fervent words, full of unction, like so many transports, or cries of the heart to God. As for example: My God, be all things to me! I desire only Thee for time and eternity; Lord, who is like unto Thee? My Lord and my God; my God, and nothing more!

12th. It must be remarked that this true simplicity makes us live in a state of continual death to self and of perfect detachment, by causing us to go with the utmost directness to God without stopping at any creature. But this grace of simplicity is not obtained by speculation, but by great purity of heart, and true mortification and contempt of self. He who avoids suffering, humiliations, and refuses to die to self, will never have any part in it. This is why there are so few who advance herein; for few indeed are willing to leave themselves, and they endure in consequence immense losses, and deprive themselves of incomprehensible blessings. O happy souls who spare nothing to belong wholly to God! Happy religious who faithfully follow all the observances of their institute! Through this fidelity they die continually to self, to their own judgment, to their own will, to their inclinations and natural repugnances, and are thus admirably though unconsciously disposed for this excellent method of prayer. There is nothing more hidden than the life of a religious who follows in all things the observances and ordinary exercises of his or her community, giving no exterior manifestation of anything extraordinary: it is a life which is a complete and continual death; through it the kingdom of God is established in us, and all other things are liberally given us.

13th. We should not neglect the reading of spiritual books; but we should read with simplicity, and in a spirit of prayer, and not through curious research. We read in a spirit of prayer when we permit the lights and sentiments revealed to us through the reading to be imprinted on our souls, and when this impression is made by the presence of God rather than by our industry.

14th. We must be armed, moreover, with two or three maxims: first, that a devout person without prayer is a body without a soul; second, that there can be no true and solid prayer without mortification, without recollection, without humility; third, that we need perseverance, never to be disheartened by the difficulties to be encountered in this exercise.

15th. It must be borne in mind that one of the greatest secrets of the spiritual life is that the Holy Spirit guides us therein, not only by lights, sweetness, consolations, and attractions, but also by obscurities, darkness, insensibility, contradictions, anguish, revolts of the passions, and inclinations. I say, moreover, that this crucified way is necessary; that it is good; that it is the surest, and that it leads us much more rapidly to perfection. An enlightened soul dearly appreciates the guidance of God, which permits her to be tried by creatures and overwhelmed with temptations and neglect; and she fully understands that these things are favors rather than misfortunes, preferring to die on the cross on Calvary than live in sweetness on Thabor. Experience will teach her in time the truth of these beautiful words: *Et nox illuminatio mea in deliciis meis; et mea nox obscurum non habet; sed omnia in luce clarescunt.* [2] The soul, after her purification in the Purgatory of suffering through which she must necessarily pass, will enjoy light, rest, and joy through intimate union with God, who will make this world, exile as it is, a paradise for her. The best prayer is that in which we most freely abandon ourselves to the sentiments and dispositions which God gives the soul, and in which we study with most simplicity, humility, and fidelity to conform ourselves to His will and to the example of Jesus Christ.

Great God, who by a series of marvellous and special circumstances didst provide from all eternity for the composition of this little work, permit not that certain minds, some of which are to be found among scholars and others among spiritual persons, ever be accused before Thy dread tribunal of having contributed in any way to close Thee the entrance to innumerable hearts, because Thou didst will to enter them in a manner the very simplicity of which shocked them, and by a way which, opened as it was by the saints since the first ages of the Church, was not yet, perhaps, sufficiently known to them: grant rather that all of us becoming as little children, as our Lord commands, we may enter upon this way, in order to teach it more safely and efficaciously to others. Amen.

---

[2] And night shall be my light in my pleasures, and my night knoweth no darkness, but all things shine in light.

IV. Exercise of Loving Union of our Will with that of God.

By St. Francis de Sales.

1st Point. Kneeling in deepest humility before the ineffable majesty of God, adore His sovereign goodness which from all eternity called you by your name, and resolved to save you, as He assures you in these words of the Prophet: "I have loved thee with an everlasting love; therefore have I drawn thee, taking pity on thee;" and destined for you, among other means, this present day, which you can employ in works of salvation and life.

2d Point. With this thought so full of truth, unite your will to that of your heavenly Father, so good and so merciful, in the following or similar words, from the depth of your heart: O sweet will of God, be ever accomplished! O eternal designs of the divine will, I adore Thee; I consecrate and dedicate my will to Thee; to ever will what Thou hast willed from all eternity. May I accomplish to-day, and always, and in all things Thy divine will, O my loving Creator! Yes, heavenly Father, according to Thy good pleasure from all eternity, and forever! Amen! O infinite Goodness, may it be as Thou hast willed! O eternal Will, live and reign in my will, now and forever!

3d Point. Invoke again the divine assistance thus: O God, come to my aid; let Thy strengthening hand confirm my poor, weak courage! Behold, O my Saviour, this poor, miserable heart has conceived, through Thy goodness, several holy affections; but alas! it is too weak and wretched to execute the good it desires. I beg the intercession of the Blessed Virgin, of my good angel, and of all the heavenly court. May their assistance be given me according to Thy good pleasure.

4th Point. Make, then, in this way a strong and loving union of your will with that of God; and in the midst of the temporal and spiritual actions of the day frequently renew this union which you have established in the morning, by simply casting an interior glance upon the divine Goodness, saying by way of acquiescence: "Yes, Lord, I wish it; yes, my Father, yes; always yes!" You can also, if you wish, make the sign of the cross, or kiss the cross of your rosary, your medal, or some pious picture; for all this will signify that you remit yourself to the Providence of God, that you adore it, that you love it with all your heart, that you unite your will irrevocably to that supreme will.

5th. But these whisperings of the heart, these interior words, should be uttered peacefully and firmly; they should be distilled, so to speak, softly and lovingly in the depths of the mind; and as we whisper in the ear of a friend a word which we desire should penetrate his heart alone, thus these whisperings will penetrate deeper and more efficaciously than these transports, these ejaculatory prayers, and these outbursts. Experience will prove this to you, provided you are humble and simple.

May God and His holy Mother be praised!

V. Act of Abandonment.

By St. Jane Frances de Chantal.

O sovereign goodness of the sovereign Providence of my God! I abandon myself forever to Thy arms. Whether gentle or severe, lead me henceforth whither Thou wilt; I will not regard the way through which Thou wilt have me pass, but keep my eyes fixed upon Thee, my God, who guidest me. My soul finds no rest without the arms and the bosom of this heavenly Providence, my true Mother, my strength and my rampart. Therefore I resolve with Thy divine assistance, O my Saviour, to follow Thy desires and Thy ordinances, without regarding or examining why Thou dost this rather than that; but I will blindly follow Thee according to Thy divine will, without seeking my own inclinations.

Hence I am determined to leave all to Thee, taking no part therein save by keeping myself in peace in Thy arms, desiring nothing except as Thou incitest me to desire, to will, to wish. I offer Thee this desire, O my God, beseeching Thee to bless it; I undertake all it includes, relying on Thy goodness, liberality, and mercy, with entire confidence in Thee, distrust of myself, and knowledge of my infinite misery and infirmity.

Another Act of Abandonment.

By Bossuet.

My God, who art goodness itself, I adore this infinite goodness; I unite myself to it, and I rely upon it, even more than upon its effects. I find no good in me, no good work done with the fidelity and perfection Thou desirest, nor anything which can make me pleasing to Thee; hence I place no trust in myself or in my works, but in Thee alone, O infinite goodness, who in one moment canst effect in me all that is needful to make me pleasing to Thee! In this belief I live; and while I live, to my last sigh, I remit my heart, my body, my mind, my soul, and my will into Thy divine hands.

O Jesus, only Son of the living God, who camest into the world to redeem my sinful soul, I abandon it to Thee! I place Thy precious blood, Thy holy death and passion, and Thy adorable wounds, and particularly that of Thy Sacred Heart, between Thy divine justice and my sins; and thus I live in the faith and hope I have in Thee, O Son of God, who hast loved me and given Thyself for me. Amen.

Another Act of Abandonment.

By Venerable Father Pignatelli.

O my God, I know not what must come to me to-day; but I am certain that nothing can happen me which Thou hast not foreseen, decreed, and ordained from all eternity: that is sufficient for me. I adore Thy impenetrable and eternal designs, to which I submit with all my heart; I desire, I accept them all, and I unite my sacrifice to that of Jesus Christ, my divine Saviour; I ask in His name, and through His infinite merits, patience in my trials, and perfect and entire submission to all that comes to me by Thy good pleasure. Amen.

By Rev. Claude De La Colombiere, S.J.

My God, I believe so firmly that Thou watchest over all who hope in Thee, and that we can want for nothing when we rely upon Thee in all things, that I am resolved for the future to have no anxieties, and to cast all my cares upon Thee. "*In peace in the self-same I will sleep and I will rest; for Thou, O Lord, singularly hast settled me in hope.*"

Men may deprive me of worldly goods and of honors; sickness may take from me my strength and the means of serving Thee; I may even lose Thy grace by sin: but my trust shall never leave me; I will preserve it to the last moment of my life, and the powers of hell shall seek in vain to wrest it from me. *"In peace in the self-same I will sleep and I will rest."*

Let others seek happiness in their wealth, in their talents; let them trust to the purity of their lives, the severity of their mortifications, to the number of their good works, the fervor of their prayers; as for me, O my God, in my very confidence lies all my hope. *"For Thou, O Lord, singularly hast settled me in hope."* This confidence can never be vain. *"No one has hoped in the Lord and has been confounded."*

I am assured, therefore, of my eternal happiness, for I firmly hope for it, and all my hope is in Thee. *"In Thee, O Lord, have I hoped; let me never be confounded."*

I know, alas! I know but too well that I am weak and unstable; I know the power of temptation against the strongest virtue. I have seen stars fall from heaven, and pillars of the firmament totter; but these things alarm me not. While I hope in Thee I am sheltered from all misfortune, and I am sure that my trust shall endure, for I rely upon Thee to sustain this unfailing hope. Finally, I know that my confidence cannot exceed Thy bounty, and that I shall never receive less than I have hoped for from Thee. Therefore I hope that Thou wilt sustain me against my evil inclinations; that Thou wilt protect me against the most furious assaults of the evil one, and that Thou wilt cause my weakness to triumph over my most powerful enemies. I hope that Thou wilt never cease to love me, and that I shall love Thee unceasingly.

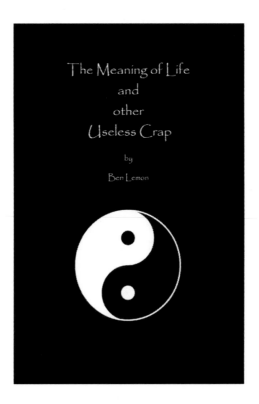

The Meaning of Life and Other Useless Crap is perhaps our generations greatest work as it answers the age old question "What is the meaning of life?" Written simply and straightforward it is easy to understand why Ben Lemon is the most important living philosopher. It hasn't been since A Modest Proposal that a pamphlet can our perceptions so dramatically.

Made in United States
North Haven, CT
06 March 2023

33659965R00070